SACAJAWEA

HANE

SACAJAWEA

Her True Story

Rich Haney

To order additional copies of this book, contact:
Xlibris Corporation
1-888-7-XLIBRIS
www.Xlibris.com
Orders@Xlibris.com

CONTENTS

CONTENTS

PROLOGUE

This is not an attempt to tell Sacajawea's life story in chronological order, because the basic facts have been enumerated many times across two centuries. Rather, I endeavor to elaborate on the reasons many white historians erroneously maintain that she died in 1812 at Fort Manuel in South Dakota, although her Shoshoni people rightfully claim she died in 1884 on Wyoming's Wind River Reservation, her final resting place.

There are more statues and memorials honoring Sacajawea than any female in American history; furthermore, a new dollar coin, debuting in March of 2000 and bearing her image, will become ubiquitous, adding to her fame and once again reminding Americans of the debt they owe her. And beyond all that, America is already gearing up for what will be a lavish bicentennial celebration, from 2003 until 2006, of the 1805-06 Lewis and Clark Expedition, which established Sacajawea as an American legend of the first order.

For an individual of such enormous significance to our history and our heritage, I believe it is ridiculous and uncalled for that some historians claim she died in South Dakota in 1812 and others maintain she died in Wyoming in 1884. And where is she buried — South Dakota or Wyoming? The historians are also divided on that issue.

It seems that America's most anointed historians — Ken Burns and Steven Ambrose — have decided that Sacajawea died in 1812 at Fort Manuel and is buried in South Dakota. Wyoming's most anointed historian — T. A. Larson — also takes that line. However, Burns, Ambrose and Larson are wrong. Sacajawea died on the Wind River Reservation in Wyoming in 1884 and there she is buried. Permit me, if you will, to prove my point in the pages of this book.

SACAJAWEA

(Poem by Porter B. Coolidge)

O Strangely sweet and darkly fair,
An Indian girl with raven hair
In silken strands of gloss and gloom
Oft mingling with the rose's bloom;
And wildly sweet the melody
Her tameless spirit sings to me.

I stooped where swift Poposia flows
And plucked for her a fresh, wild rose;
Her dark gaze cast a snowy rim
With twilight's purple shadows dim;
Then softly, quaintly she did sing
Like bird at eve with folded wing.

Now sunset's golden dreams are dead.
The Indian girl from me hath fled;
Still linger in the star-lit skies
The dusk and splendor of her eyes;
And voice of distant waterfall
Sweet echoes of her song recall.

***

CHAPTER ONE

At the beginning of the nineteenth century, President Thomas Jefferson was concerned about America's growth as long as European countries held large North American territories. In 1800 Spain ceded the vast Louisiana Territory to France, which had become a dominant military power under Napoleon Bonaparte.

Napoleon needed cash to finance his military ventures in Europe, a situation that Jefferson quickly exploited. With James Monroe and Robert Livingston as his negotiators, Jefferson gave Napoleon $15 million for the Louisiana Territory, doubling the size of the United States.

The purchase dazzled Jefferson's vivid imagination. He claimed that the territory extended from the Mississippi River to the Rocky Mountains but even the French didn't dispute the fact that, perhaps, it extended all the way to the Pacific Ocean.[1]

Jefferson was immediately enchanted with devising an exploratory expedition that would survey his expansive and uncharted land. He sent his personal secretary, Lieutenant Meriwether Lewis, to Philadelphia to study astronomy, zoology and botany. Then he named Lewis and Captain William Clark to head the expedition, which left St. Louis in May of 1804.[2]

While plans of expanding America and extricating its borders from the stifling control of European powers began to consume the astute and visionary President Jefferson, another event was taking place a world away, on the Great Plains that were shadowed by the eastern flanks of the foreboding Rocky Mountains. A rival Indian tribe attacked and destroyed a Shoshoni encampment, killing most of its inhabitants but making sure to capture prized Shoshoni girls, who would become slaves or trade bait for French-

Canadian trappers. In that manner, a eleven-year-old Shoshoni girl became a slave and was bartered about among various tribes for several years.

This Indian girl's name was Sacajawea.[3]

At about age thirteen, in 1803, she was sold by the Minataree Indians to a French-Canadian trapper named Toussaint Charbonneau, who was about thirty-two years her senior. Charbonneau had a fetish for little Indian girls and, into his eighties, he would collect them to be his "wives." So, Sacajawea — a name that meant "one who launches boats" — went from slavery to bondage as she entered her teens.[4]

Even for a little Indian girl on the Great Plains, Sacajawea had it especially rough. And yet, while still a teenager, she would perform deeds with such grace and dignity that she would emerge as the most honored female in the history of America. And I speak of an America that, partially thanks to her, was destined to become the greatest, most powerful and richest nation in the history of the entire world.

And so, one nexus for America's leap toward greatness was hatched early in the nineteenth century with Thomas Jefferson's Louisiana Purchase and the survival of a little Indian girl on the Great Plains. The two seminal events would incredibly merge and in the next two centuries more statues and memorials would honor that little Indian girl than any female in America's history. Incredibly, she was instrumental in making Jefferson's astonishing vision a success.

Now, as the twenty-first century dawns, the much-anticipated Sacajawea dollar coin will make her name and image considerably more prestigious around America and around the world. That coin bears the date "2000" and then, with America's very lavish bicentennial celebration of the Lewis and Clark Expedition set for 2003 until 2006, Sacajawea's status as the superstar of that momentous event will be documented, over and over. The little Indian girl, already the most honored female in America's history, will become even more famous.

Sacajawea, of course, never anticipated or sought such ever-lasting fame, although she earned it and deserves it. One thing she did not earn and does not deserve is the controversy that has raged for almost two centuries concerning when and where she died and where she is buried. Did she die in South Dakota in 1812 or in Wyoming in 1884?

Is she buried near the South Dakota—North Dakota border or is she buried on the Wind River Reservation in Wyoming?

Many of America's most noted historians maintain that Sacajawea died in South Dakota in 1812 and is buried there. But the United States Government and Sacajawea's own Shoshoni people claim she died on Wyoming's Wind River Reservation in 1884 and that remains her final resting place.

For an individual of such enormous importance to American history, the disparity is truly astounding and, I think, uncalled for.

Inherently elusive except around trusted friends and family members, Sacajawea remains unfathomable to some and paradoxical to many. Life's vexations still lurk for this most idyllic of characters, as a rash of historical revisionists strive to shorten her life by seventy-two years. Each new stride for the Sacajawea legend, such as the year 2000 Dollar Coin, spawns a conundrum for her Shoshoni people, who must endure fresh inanities relating to her supposed 1812 death.

Therefore, I will herewith strive to answer, hopefully to your satisfaction, the again very topical question of where and when the icon named Sacajawea died and where she is buried.

CHAPTER TWO

It seems that South Dakota has more vigorously and successfully claimed the final resting place of Sacajawea than often-dismissed Wyoming has managed to do. For example, famed video-historian Ken Burns and noted writer-historian Steven Ambrose — in their recently celebrated PBS documentary on the Lewis and Clark Expedition — quite summarily concluded that Sacajawea died in 1812 at Fort Manuel and is buried in South Dakota.[5]

Even the most noted Wyoming historians, such as T. A. Larson, have capitulated to the South Dakota claims.[6]

Indeed, history records that John C. Luttig, a clerk at Fort Manuel in South Dakota, wrote these words in his journal on the twentieth of December, 1812: "This evening the wife of Charbonneau, a Snake Squaw, died of a putrid fever. She was the best woman in the fort, aged about 25 years. She left a fine infant girl."[7]

To the white world, when Luttig's quotation was spread by newspapers and word of mouth, this meant that Sacajawea had died on December 20th, 1812, at Fort Manuel in South Dakota. After all, Charbonneau's "Snake Squaw" on the 1805—1806 Lewis and Clark Expedition was Sacajawea. Overlooked or dismissed in much of the white culture was the basic fact that Charbonneau, a rogue, usually had multiple Indian "wives," often two or more at the same time. Most of them were usually purchased by Charbonneau from their Indian captors, as were Sacajawea and another Shoshoni named Otter Woman. And Luttig's description of the "Snake Squaw aged about 25 years" that died at Fort Manuel perfectly fit Otter Woman, the Charbonneau "wife" that actually died at Fort Manuel on December 20th, 1812.

For years thereafter, much of the white world continued to accept as fact that Sacajawea had died in 1812 at Fort Manuel. However, the Indian world that clearly understood the distinction between Sacajawea and Otter Woman well knew that it was Otter Woman that died in 1812 and that Sacajawea, who was in St. Louis at the time, still lived.[8]

John Tarnese, my full-blooded Shoshoni friend and an expert on the Oral or Traditional History of the Shoshones, says, "In the years 1806 to 1820, or right after the Lewis and Clark journey till her final split with Charbonneau, Sacajawea made forays back and forth from St. Louis, where she and her two sons were befriended by Captain William Clark, to the Indian world. She was happiest among Indians but she loved Clark and respected his power, that is his ability to make life better for Baptiste and Basil, her sons. Her relationship with Charbonneau had changed and she now used him more than he used her. At least twice during this period she used his fur-trade connections to get back and forth from St. Louis to the Plains. She no longer tolerated one of his habits, which was to mistreat his 'wives' on whims. It was the spring of 1820 when, on the edge of St. Louis, he sided with a Ute 'wife' nicknamed Eagle and the argument resulted in Charbonneau's beating Sacajawea. But she secured a hatchet and chased him outside, shouting that she would kill him or he'd have to kill her if they ever met up again. They didn't. The Shoshones, the Comanches and the Gros Ventres, in three different areas that are now three different states, all knew Sacajawea during this period. She had some good moments with Clark in St. Louis but mostly moped around the streets otherwise, 'cause she was out of her element. The white world, at the time, was confused about Otter Woman's death at Fort Manuel in 1812, some segments believing it was Sacajawea, but mostly the whites didn't care one way or the other. And the Shoshones, of course, saw no need to enlighten them because they weren't asked and because the two cultures were so different anyway. Meanwhile, Sacajawea spent two teary winter months with Clark in St. Louis in 1821. The tears were because, with her sons

now adults and taken care of . . . Baptiste had gone to Europe and
Basil preferred the Plains . . . she told Clark that she, too, must
forever return to her people, and without the tugs of wanting to
see him again. In the spring of 1821 Sacajawea said her last good-
bye to Clark, reminding him that she had no more such good-
byes in her. He understood, knowing that the feral colt he loved
now needed to be turned back to the wild. After a political speech
in Omaha . . . we believe it was the summer of 1825 . . . Clark
was asked a lot of political questions because he was an important
government man then. But he was also asked, 'Sacajawea, Mister
Clark . . . where is she, how is she?' He put his face in his hands
and closed his eyes for a minute or so. Then he looked up and said
just two words: 'She's happy.' Tears in his eyes punctuated those
two words and thus there were no more questions about Sacajawea.
And how did the Shoshones learn of that teary answer in Omaha?
Mormons were there because they attended many of William Clark's
political appearances because he was a powerful man regarding
how the government treated both Mormons and Indians. And
many Mormon missionaries frequented Shoshoni encampments.
That's how our Oral History registers that teary, two-word sentence — "She's happy" — from William Clark, long after part of
the white world was believing that Sacajawea had died at Fort
Manuel in 1812."

And then, in 1826, Captain William Clark was asked to reveal
the whereabouts of the members of the famed 1805-1806 expedition. He wrote these words on the first page of that journal: "Se car
ja we au — Dead." This, in some white minds, merely reaffirmed
that the now legendary Sacajawea had indeed died in 1812 at Fort
Manuel, because the white person known to be extremely close to
Sacajawea, during and after the expedition, was the greatly respected William Clark.[9]

Still, during this period and for decades afterward, the Indian
world knew that Sacajawea was alive, and she was the Sacajawea
now famed in the white world as the celebrated heroine of the
Lewis and Clark Expedition.

Sacajawea was quite modest and, true to her nature and culture, she was not one to brag about her exploits with Lewis and Clark. Also, any bragging would have been met with cold shoulders anywhere in the world of the Plains Indians, who considered the Lewis and Clark thing strictly a white phenomenon, if they bothered to consider it at all.

Indeed, U. S. politicians and officials who recently selected Sacajawea from a long list to be the honoree on the upcoming dollar coin were stunned that some Indian groups were the first to oppose her nomination. Why? Because some Native Americans still resent or at least lament the fact that Sacajawea's fame is based on something she did for whites, not for Indians.

In this milieu, in the decades prior to her death in 1884, Sacajawea lived a quiet and dignified life back in her own Shoshoni culture in the territory that became the state of Wyoming in 1890.

If much of the white world was misinformed, the Indian world was not. They knew exactly who Sacajawea was and so did many, many white missionaries who interacted very closely with the Plains Indians. Campfire stories, not misinformation from newspapers or from word of mouth in the white world, informed the Plains Indians of Sacajawea's unique renown but this did not make her a heroine among her own people. The Sacajawea her own people knew spoke very fluent French. She carried a sack around with her that contained little mementos of the Lewis and Clark Expedition, mementos that only Sacajawea could have owned and accurately associated with the Lewis and Clark Expedition. And she very proudly wore around her neck a Thomas Jefferson Medal that was given to her, and to her alone, by the grateful United States Government.[10]

"But understand," Tarnese said, "her renown in the white world — the truths and the untruths — didn't matter to the Plains Indians. It did matter that she had settled back with her own people. She was soon happily married to a Comanche brave named Jirk Meat. The Comanches were cousins of the Shoshones and spoke the same tongue. It never crossed Sacajawea's mind, or the

Indians' minds, to exploit her fame in the white world. Rather, it was down-played. However, there was no doubt among the various Indian tribes about who she was. The medals and such, keepsakes from her Lewis and Clark travels, were intriguing, resulting in campfire stories that she partook in, but only when asked to do so. Starting with the Comanches, she was given a series of four or five nicknames, as was customary for Indian women. The Comanche nickname 'Porivo' meant 'Chief Woman' and directly referred to the fame they knew she had in the white world. When Mormon missionaries flocked among the Plains Indians, little comments alerted them to Sacajawea and a problem arose about that pipeline of information flowing back to the whites. Missionaries who made too much of that white fame were cut off or siphoned out of any close attachments to the Sacajawea-inhabited encampments. There was, you see, jealousy among the Plains Indians that the whites were trying to usurp, or claim, one of their own, and to do so under a pretext, the Lewis and Clark journey, that didn't much interest them at all."

And so, proud of her memories from the Lewis and Clark days — especially the remembrances of William Clark and her attachment to the Jefferson Medal she wore around her neck — Sacajawea was safely back in her own world by the mid-1820s. Over in the white world, the rumors that she had died at Fort Manuel in 1812 didn't cause much of a stir because there was no mechanism, such as an all-encompassing and cohesive media, to highlight her mounting fame. That would be left to the history books, which spawned the great influx of statues during the second half of the nineteenth century. Only then did Sacajawea's intoxicating persona, coupled with her unquestioned devotion and value to the Lewis and Clark Expedition, begin to make her a legend of the first order in the white world. But it was not until the Twentieth Century, when the full bore of both the printed and electronic media converged, that the primary questions concerning when and where she died began to play fully with the Sacajawea legend. The fact that America, especially the media, was so infantile in 1812, when the first rumor emerged about her death, explains why the question was not more readily scrutinized then, which would have been the more appropriate time. The United States Government, in fact, waited until 1925 to fund a major investigation into when and where Sacajawea died, and where she was buried. That investigation revealed that she died in 1884 in Wyoming but, because it was so long overdue, it left plenty of room for pundits and skeptics to not let go of, or to build on, the rumor that she, not Otter Woman, died in 1812 at Fort Manuel.

Since the famed 1812 Tom Luttig note, the controversy as to when and where Sacajawea died has been on a cyclical roller-coaster ride for almost two centuries. Dr. Grace Raymond Hebard — a noted University of Wyoming librarian, attorney and historian — began an extensive study of Sacajawea in the early 1900s and by 1907 Dr. Hebard had settled on the theory that Sacajawea died on April ninth, 1884, on the Wind River Reservation in Wyoming. Dr. Hebard became obsessed with the Sacajawea legend and devoted most of her adult life to researching it, chronicling her findings in the 1932 book entitled Sacajawea: A Guide and Interpreter of the Lewis and Clark Expedition.

Born in Clinton, Iowa, in 1861, Dr. Hebard died in Laramie, Wyoming, in 1936.[11] For the last three decades of her life, Dr. Hebard's conclusion that Sacajawea died in 1884 on Wyoming's Wind River Reservation ruled the historical roost. But after Dr. Hebard's death, Wyoming historians T. A. Larson and Blanche Schroer learned in the 1940s that one of William Clark's heirs had discovered a journal in which Clark wrote, in the year of 1826, these words: "Se ca ja wea Dead." As I will examine later, Larson and Schroer pounced on that notation William Clark scribbled in his messy 1826 journal, two words that convinced Larson, Schroer and many others that Sacajawea did indeed die at Fort Manuel in 1812.[12] Thus, the vacillating pendulum swung back to the 1812 theory of Sacajawea's death, even among the leading Wyoming historians.

However, the greatest of all Sacajawea historians remains Dr.

Grace Raymond Hebard. Her 1884 version of Sacajawea's death on Wyoming's Wind River Reservation is supported by Sacajawea's own close-knit people, the Shoshones, and by the U. S. Government, which funded an extensive investigation in 1925.[13]

Blanche Schroer, on Page twenty-three of her long essay entitled Sacajawea: The Legend and the Truth, wrote: "At present, Dr. T. A. Larson, an historian who has both a comprehensive knowledge of United States and Wyoming history, and is a member of the Wyoming Legislature, has been protecting us from obtaining a national monument (dedicated to Sacajawea) under false pretenses. The further difficulty is that Dr. Hebard, perhaps half-innocently, created a legend. And legends die hard."

Yes, legends do die hard. But Dr. Hebard didn't create the Sacajawea legend; she merely researched it better than anyone else, including Schroer, Larson, Burns and Ambrose. Sacajawea was Dr. Hebard's lifelong passion and only after her death in 1936 has she been pilloried for her historical conclusions, which I deem to be essentially correct. The discovery in the 1940s of the 1826 William Clark notation — "Se ca ja wea Dead" — simply does not discredit Dr. Hebard's magnificent research or the findings of Dr. Charles Eastman in his federally funded investigation, not to mention the decades-long consistency of the Shoshoni people who knew Sacajawea best.

CHAPTER THREE

From time to time, well into her nineties, Sacajawea regaled her own people and extremely well educated white missionaries and preachers with meticulous and corroborated details of the Lewis and Clark Expedition, details that only Sacajawea could have known.[14]

The Indians, the missionaries and the preachers who knew Sacajawea from 1812 till 1884 as the Lewis and Clark heroine could not possibly have been totally mistaken. Neither then nor now could such a hoax have been perpetrated and surely the Plains Indians, who couldn't relate to the white man's thirst for fame and fortune, had neither the incentive nor the means to engage in such chicanery.

Could someone have fabricated a Sacajawea that spoke fluent French? Would that fabrication have possessed many small but verified mementos belonging only to the Lewis and Clark heroine?

Would a fake Sacajawea have been the sole owner of the Jefferson Medal the U. S. Government gave to Sacajawea?

Would a make-believe Sacajawea have been able to reminisce about minor and major details of the Lewis and Clark Expedition, infallible details that were later corroborated by mesmerized missionaries?

Could some incredibly elaborate scheme in that era have created a replica of Sacajawea that would have fooled her own people as well as the missionaries that knew her intimately?

Did William Clark make a mistake in 1826 when he wrote those words: "Se car ja we au — Dead?" No, he was probably not mistaken; he most likely lied, to lay down some subterfuge for Sacajawea. From the first moment he saw her, Clark was in awe of

Sacajawea and very soon and very permanently he was in love with her. He held back the expedition to personally help birth the teenage Sacajawea's baby, Baptiste. Clark was verily smitten with the baby, whom he nicknamed Pomp, which was also what Sacajawea called him. In his diaries and in conversations, Clark often called Pomp "my son" or "my boy." In fact, some historians maintained that Clark, not Charbonneau, actually sired Pomp, the famed "papoose" depicted in the cradleboard on Sacajawea's back in the countless statues and paintings and on the upcoming dollar coin.[15]

While eight of the thirty-one members of the expedition kept meticulous diaries, it was Clark's renderings that made Sacajawea an American heroine of the first order. He could not and would not let go of her when the expedition ended. Back in St. Louis he begged her to get shed of the rogue Charbonneau and he promised to shower her, Pomp and her newly adopted son Basil with whatever they needed or desired. Sacajawea, unquestionably a fiercely loving and protective mother, wanted Pomp educated in the white world. Clark, of course, complied and made sure that Pomp got superbly educated both in America and in Europe.

Sacajawea, purchased as a slave by Charbonneau, never loved the roving Frenchman, who beat her and taunted her about his many other "wives." It is known that one of his other "wives" — Eagle —was very jealous of Sacajawea and continually urged Charbonneau to mistreat her. Otter Woman, the Charbonneau "wife" that died at Fort Manuel in 1812, was actually the only one that Sacajawea liked and tolerated. That's why Clark himself adopted the infant daughter that Otter Woman left behind at Fort Manuel.[16]

Sacajawea, on the famed Corps of Discovery, fell in love with Clark and spent most of her time with him and his Negro servant York, whom she was sexually attracted to. When Otter Woman and Charbonneau made the trip upriver to Fort Manuel in 1812, Sacajawea was with Clark in St. Louis. But his world was not her world. She wanted Pomp, at his tender age, to begin reaping the benefits of the white world but she longed to return to her own culture and the comfort zone of the Plains Indians. There is nothing that William Clark would not have done for Sacajawea and he acquiesced to her wishes. He knew that she merely wanted to blend back in with the Shoshones and their Plains Indian brethren and that she did not want to be hounded by her mounting fame in the white world. Thus, William Clark was in a position that can be equated with a young man who had rescued a feral colt, tamed him and loved him but one day realized the colt needed to be turned loose back into the wild. William Clark loved Sacajawea enough to finally let go of her, undoubtedly with tears in his eyes and in her eyes.

And so, like a feral colt, he turned her loose, and later registered that lie, or mistake, in 1826 to continue to cover her tracks.[17]

The Sacajawea that William Clark and the Plains Indians knew so well, and the Sacajawea that would forever be a legend in the white world, returned to the Shoshoni people that she knew as a girl, ending up in what is now the Green River area of Wyoming.

She fell in love with a Comanche/Shoshonean brave named Jirk Meat and was his loving wife for twenty-six years, bearing him five children. Jirk Meat, on the saddest day of Sacajawea's life, was killed in a skirmish with a rival tribe. She covered her dwelling with straw, indicating that she could live there no more. With the quiet dignity that had always been one of her indelible trademarks, Sacajawea then lived in Shoshoni encampments along the Wind River in Wyoming.

After his sojourn to Europe, Pomp spent considerable time in the West but he was only reunited with his mother on two significant occasions. The well-educated Pomp could now speak five languages fluently and no longer could he deeply identify with a mother who was thoroughly a Shoshone.

But Basil, Sacajawea's beloved adopted son, worshipped his mother and was with her constantly. As Sacajawea entered her nineties on the Wind River, she lived with Basil and his family and they tenderly cared for her.[18]

On April ninth, 1884, Sacajawea died as Basil kissed her hand and whispered to her. With tears in his eyes, Basil informed Indian Agent Lane that, "My mother is dead." Lane, who knew Sacajawea well, reported for posterity that he watched her body being wrapped in skins and sewed for burial. Then Lane said he was there when her body was placed on her favorite horse, which Basil led to a mourning site.[19] Indian accounts starkly confirm what Indian Agent Lane stated.

The Reverend John Roberts and three other well respected white ministers officiated at Sacajawea's burial in the cemetery at Fort Washakie, Wyoming. All those ministers knew Sacajawea well and knew her to be the heroine of the Lewis and Clark Expedition. They watched as Basil held back the burial "for the longest time" as he insisted on saying his final good-bye with "a thousand kisses."[20]

CHAPTER FOUR

So who was Sacajawea and why is she so special? Why is she the most memorialized female in American history? Why, almost two centuries after her exploits with the Lewis and Clark Expedition, is she being further honored with her image on the most anticipated American coin in many decades? And why, with the upcoming bicentennial celebration of the Lewis and Clark Expedition, will Americans be reminded time and again of the contributions this Indian girl made to the storied history of the United States of America?

Sacajawea was born, about the year 1790, into a band of Northern Shoshones in what is now the state of Idaho. In 1800, when she was about ten, her people were camped at Three Forks, where the headwaters of the Missouri River converge in what is now southwestern Montana. Their camp was attacked and destroyed by a war party of Hidatsa Indians, Shoshoni enemies who often raided peaceful villages in order to capture horses and Shoshoni girls. The Hidatsas captured Sacajawea and they are the ones who named her, and to them "Sacajawea" meant "Bird Woman" while to the Shoshones the name very closely resembled their word for "one who launches boats."[21]

At the time, Toussaint Charbonneau, a French-Canadian fur trapper, lived among the Hidatsas. As was his custom, Charbonneau purchased pretty Indian girls as his own "toys" and, when the prettiest ones came of age, he often took them as his "wives." Two captured Shoshoni girls — Sacajawea and Otter Woman — were bought by Charbonneau from the Hidatsas at about the same time.[22]

Late in 1804, the fourteen-year-old Sacajawea was pregnant with

Charbonneau's child. At that time the Lewis and Clark Expedition was in winter quarters near the villages of the Hidatsas and their neighbors, the Mandans. Lewis and Clark had been commissioned by President Jefferson to explore the uncharted land that extended westward from the upper Missouri River to the Columbia River and to the Pacific Ocean. Jefferson, although his $15 million Louisiana Purchase had taken care of French claims to the area, still worried about the claims of England, Spain and Russia to the region that was deemed vital for America's expansion westward.[2 3]

Planning to resume their journey in the spring of 1805, Lewis and Clark hired Charbonneau as an interpreter although he had with him at the time his favorite "wife," the very pregnant teenager Sacajawea.

William Clark actually conducted a marriage ceremony to unite Charbonneau and Sacajawea more officially, believing it would send a message to the twenty-eight other white men who would be in the entourage that would include the one young female.

Lewis and Clark held up the journey because Sacajawea's first born was a tough delivery. In fact, Lewis and Clark painstakingly concocted a potion — rattlesnake rattles pounded into powder and then made into a liquid — for her to swallow to speed the delivery. It worked and within ten minutes after drinking the potion Sacajawea gave birth to a son, named Jean-Baptiste.

During the birthing process, William Clark — the handsome, thirty-five-year-old explorer — began to fall in love with Sacajawea.[2 4]

He nicknamed her baby "Pomp," which meant "first born" in Shoshoni, and that's what Sacajawea also called him.

From the beginning, to illustrate his fondness for Sacajawea, Clark quite often referred to her papoose as "my son" or "my boy."

On April 7th, 1805, the Lewis and Clark Expedition broke camp and proceeded up the Missouri in six boats, four of which were really just canoes equipped with sails. There were thirty-three people in the party, including Sacajawea and her baby, Jean-Baptiste, who rode in a cradleboard on her back.

From the very first day, Sacajawea proved her mettle and her value to the troupe. She never complained about anything and her sense of adventure quickly established her abiding concern for the mission. By the journey's second day, diaries already were recording that Sacajawea, at night, would go out and dig up edible roots and extract artichokes and tubers from gopher holes. She would gladly share the nutritious vegetables with the men, even before she herself would eat. Within days, the diaries were filled with notes about how "valuable," "resourceful," "unselfish" and "inspirational" Sacajawea was. And all the men were exceptionally impressed with Sacajawea's tender mothering of her infant baby. Her demeanor, personality and purposefulness was making her the superstar of the entire troupe, right from the beginning.

A squall hit the lead boat in eastern Montana and valuable equipment spilled overboard, including instruments, medicine, journals and trade goods. Enmeshed in raging water above her waist, and with Baptiste in the cradleboard on her back, it was Sacajawea who saved the valuable equipment. Meriwether Lewis, in his journal that night, told all about how Sacajawea had salvaged "almost every article indispensable to our enterprise."[25]

Within days of setting out, Lewis also wrote that they had named a tributary of the Missouri after Sacajawea to honor her "fortitude and resolution."

The sheer speed with which this little Indian girl, saddled with the twenty-four-hour care of her first infant, established herself as the shining light of the male-dominated Lewis and Clark Expedition attests to how special she was. William Clark had already fallen in love with her, and so would all of America when its citizens learned how she had taken this young country by the hand and led it so bravely and so resolutely westward.

CHAPTER FIVE

By 1924, well over a century after the Journey of Discovery, there were more statues and paintings of Sacajawea than any other female in American history. Of all American females, none was admired as much as Sacajawea, because of the deed she had performed for this nation and because of her untarnished reputation as the quintessential mother.[26]

However, some of the statues and the history books claimed she died at Fort Manuel in 1812 and other statues and history books said she died at Fort Washakie in 1884. Some smart members in the U. S. Congress thought the disparity was ridiculous concerning a person so vital to this country's heritage.[27]

Therefore, Congress passed a resolution to get to the bottom of the quagmire, and backed that resolution with the money to fund an intense investigation. Then, on December thirteenth, 1924, the U. S. Department of the Interior instructed a blue-ribbon commission to mount that investigation and report back to Congress.[28]

The investigation was headed by a diligent and respected Indian expert named Charles A. Eastman. On March second, 1925, Eastman filed his definitive report with the Department of Interior and the U. S. Congress, a ten-page, typed report that included a plethora of other documentation and exhibits. I include at the end of this book an exact copy of Eastman's ten-page summation of his findings.

As you will see, Eastman states that "the Shoshone woman who died at Fort Manuel was Otter Woman, the other Shoshone wife of Charbonneau." And Eastman states conclusively, "Basil, the oldest son, or her step son whom she raised and called her own son, was exceptionally devoted to her. It was in his family that she (Sacajawea) lived and died." And Eastman added, with authority and without equivocation, "She died April 9, 1884, and was buried by Missionary Roberts at Fort Washakie, Wyoming."

The very last sentence of Eastman's report stresses that "I report that Sacajawea died on April 9, 1884, at Fort Washakie, Wyoming, her final resting place."

Many anointed historians — including Ken Burns, Steven Ambrose and T. A. Larson — have gone off on wild goose chases to dispute the Eastman report to the U. S. Government in 1925. I do not consider myself an historian but for forty-five years — or since I was enchanted with a Sacajawea statue in my hometown, Thomas Jefferson's Charlottesville, Virginia — I have meticulously studied her life, including the opinions of Burns, Ambrose and Larson. They are wrong and Eastman is correct concerning Otter Woman's death at Fort Manuel in 1812 and Sacajawea's death at Fort Washakie in 1884.

As Sacajawea's reputation continued to soar, another U. S. Congress had a propitious thought: "If Sacajawea is such a giant in our history books, why don't we fund a major and suitable memorial for her near her burial site in Wyoming?" There was no opposition to that Congressional plan to federally fund and federally perpetuate a major memorial for Sacajawea on the Wind River Reservation, except from the state of Wyoming itself.[29]

It so happened at the time that Wyoming's anointed historian, Taft Alfred Larson, was also a key member of the Wyoming legislature and Mr. Larson had decided that Sacajawea did not die and was not buried on the Wind River Reservation. He said that if Wyoming was the recipient of such a federally funded and maintained memorial that it would be under "false pretenses."[30]

The U. S. Congress was befuddled, still very much believing the Eastman report but deciding that, if Wyoming didn't want that lush memorial, why should it bother? And so, to this day, no such memorial exists in Wyoming. I sincerely believe that is an injustice to America, to Wyoming and, most of all, to Sacajawea.

T. A. Larson, who was born in 1910 and is still alive, has lived in Wyoming since 1936 and is the author of the comprehensive *History of Wyoming*, which won the American Association for State and Local History Award of Merit in 1966. He is a great man and a fine citizen of Wyoming, but I believe he has done a great disservice to the memory of Sacajawea, and to the State of Wyoming.

In his book entitled *Wyoming, A History*, which was published worldwide by New York-and-London-based W. W. Norton & Company, Mr. Larson tells us all about a Shoshoni woman named Madam Jack Robinson. Her claim to fame, apparently, was that she was married to "one of Jim Bridger's trappers." But in the entire book there is nary a mention of Sacajawea.[31]

In regards to Sacajawea, Mr. Larson has been quite influential, and not just with the U. S. Congress. I believe America's two highest profile historians of today — Steven Ambrose and Ken Burns — merely followed the Larson line about where and when she died. And so have many others.

I have particularly scoured the writings of the anti-Wyoming Sacajawea historians. For example, a lady named Blanche Schroer was a noted Wyoming historian who once lived on the Wind River Reservation and actually directed visitors to Sacajawea's grave in its Indian Cemetery during the 1930s. Schroer firmly believed that Sacajawea died on the Wind River in 1884, until she learned of the 1826 William Clark notation: *"Se car ja we ar — Dead."*[32] Then Schroer sided with Larson and heaped glowing praise on him for blocking the Congressional effort to gift Wyoming with that major memorial.[33]

Schroer wrote, "Dr. Larson . . . has been protecting us from obtaining a monument under false pretenses. We need more scholarly people of this type in our government."

Schroer also excoriated a fine University of Wyoming historian, Dr. Grace Raymond Hebard, for supposedly perpetuating Sacajawea's ties to Wyoming very early in this century, "beginning in 1904" with her famous Sacajawea lectures and her outstanding book that was entitled *Sacajawea*.

Also, Schroer denigrated the Daughters of the American Revolution because that organization in 1963 put a nice monument over Sacajawea's Wyoming grave, a monument engraved with these words: "Sacajawea, died April 9, 1884, A Guide with the Lewis and Clark Expedition 1805-1806, Identified by Rev. J. Roberts who officiated at her burial." Schroer wrote, "Before these women assumed such a great responsibility, they should have seriously researched the matter."

T. A. Larson and, to a lesser extent, Blanche Schroer have, I believe, unfairly muddied the waters and fanned the flames of a controversy that should not be controversial at all. The impact of Larson and Schroer is derived largely from the fact they are identified as "Wyoming historians."

Regarding Sacajawea, the oral histories of the Shoshones should be afforded at least as much currency as the white historians who largely garner their data from white newspapers and white government accounts. It was a white man at Fort Manuel, not the Shoshones, who got Otter Woman confused with Sacajawea. It was white historians, not the Shoshones, who went off on tangents regarding the Indian name Porivo, which was a nickname — meaning "Chief" — that close friends sometimes attached to Sacajawea. Thus, Schroer and others vehemently claimed that an old Shoshoni lady named Porivo, not Sacajawea, died on the Wind River Reservation on April ninth, 1884.

For any white historian that cared to listen, the Shoshones have pointed out that, over the decades, there were a lot of nicknames for Sacajawea, including Wadze-Wipe, which meant "Lost Woman;" Booe-nive, which meant "Grass Maiden;" and Bah-Ribo, which meant "Water White Man." It was typical in the Shoshoni culture for women to receive multiple names during their lifetimes.[34] White historians who didn't understand this aspect of the Shoshoni culture, and there were and are many, were and are ripe to cultivate their mistakes about Sacajawea. Many times, in depth, I have discussed this with full-blooded Shoshoni friends such as John Tarnese, who lived for many years on the Wind River Reservation within sight of Sacajawea's grave and was a longtime Shoshoni council-member.

It even appears that the Shoshones, more than the whites, understood Sacajawea's love affair with William Clark, thus better comprehending why he would be inclined to help smooth her total immersion back into Shoshoni society.

Realms of Clark's written and spoken words, recorded for history, verily drip with his awe and love of Sacajawea.[35] At the very end of the journey, Clark marveled over her, not over such things as having reached the Pacific Ocean. He said, "She is the shining star who has borne with a patience truly admirable the fatigues of so long a route, encumbered with the charge of an infant, who is even now only 19 months old."

But historic records also repeatedly reveal Sacajawea's love for Clark, not to mention their intimate togetherness during and after the expedition.[36] When Clark was nearly starving, she lied to get him to eat food that had been hoarded for her, convincing him that she had already eaten. When Clark eagerly but unsuccessfully tried to trade a coastal Indian out of a coveted sea-otter robe, Sacajawea stepped forward and swapped her prized blue-beaded belt for the robe, then presented it to Clark. At Christmas, she gifted Clark with two dozen white weasel tails.

Not only did he play a pivotal role in birthing her baby, he made sure he was by her side every possible moment. When they finally reached the Pacific, Clark even held back in camp to be with Sacajawea while most of the others surveyed the ocean's shoreline.

With sweet feistiness, she demurred with these words, "I have traveled a great way with us to see the great water, yet you do not take me down to the coast, and the others tell me of the really monstrous fish they have seen. It seems hard that you not permit me to see either the coast or the monstrous fish."[37]

Clark smiled broadly at her stance and then took her to the shore, where she saw whales, including one that was beached on the sand.

In the spring of 1806, as they returned east, Lewis took one group and Clark led the other in different routes over the Montana Rockies, then they rendezvoused on the Missouri. For sure, Clark was not separated from Sacajawea.

Eight members of the expedition — Captains Lewis and Clark; Privates Joseph Whitehouse, Robert Frazier and George Shannon; and Sergeants Charles Floyd, Patrick Gass and John Ordway — all kept diaries on the journey and all of them registered awe of Sacajawea.

The Patrick Gass journals were actually the first to be nationally published, in 1807. Lewis, before he died in 1809, never quite finalized a publishing deal but Clark, in Philadelphia in 1814, signed over the "Lewis and Clark journals" to a national publisher, J. B. Lippincott & Company.

The pragmatic Lewis heralded her exceptional intelligence and diligence such as the time she saved vital medicine, navigational instruments and historic records and guidelines that ended up in dangerously choppy water. Lewis believed the troupe would have starved had Sacajawea not done such things as craft a perfect stick to dig down in gopher holes to raid the supplies of edible vegetation that she knew the little animals hoarded. When the waters were shallow and the expedition desperately needed horses to go overland, Sacajawea greatly impressed Lewis by securing horses from two Indian tribes.

When hostile Indians threatened to wipe out the helpless troupe, it was Sacajawea with the papoose on her back who intervened.[38]

Clark and the other primary diary-keepers were even more impressed with Sacajawea's beauty, personality and demeanor. She was totally unselfish and never once complained about any hardship. Her girlish enchantments were forever recorded and remembered, such as when she danced and sang with joy when she discovered her brother, a Shoshoni chief named Cameahwait, on the journey. And they all marveled over Sacajawea's loving and unremitting devotion to her baby, Pomp.[39]

Not only was Sacajawea vital to the expedition that was vital
to President Jefferson and the entire nation, but her character and
spirit still inspires this nation. Without her, that journey would
likely have failed and America might still be contesting the French,
English, Spanish or Russians for the land stretching from the Mississippi to the Pacific Ocean.

In modern times, as we often search for "role models" amid a
vast multitude of greedy, millionaire entertainment and sports
heroes, we might glance up at a statue of Sacajawea and behold a
true role model, the one with the papoose on her back.

Being a slave girl and being purchased by a rogue didn't deter
her. No American, native or otherwise, left behind larger or more
beautiful footprints on this nation's landscape than did Sacajawea.

Therefore, I think it is essential that white historians finally
reach a consensus with the Shoshoni people themselves and with
the United States Government as to when and where Sacajawea
died, and where she is buried. I realize that one modern nuance —
television — is a giant, prohibiting factor. If an anointed historian
such as Ken Burns or Steven Ambrose has a new project to promote, even so-called T-V "news" programs will readily pimp their
material. If a Burns or an Ambrose says, "Sacajawea died in 1812
and is buried in South Dakota," never expect even that "news"
program to counter with a question such as, "But the Shoshoni
people themselves and the only federally funded government investigation maintain that she died in 1884 and is buried in Wyoming. Any comment?" That simple and appropriate question will
never be asked of a Burns or an Ambrose because it would be
embarrassing. After all, they consented to be interviewed only so
the "news" networks or the "news" papers would pimp both their
new projects and their unchallenged opinions.

In Sacajawea's case, I believe, it is time anointed historians
were indeed challenged, and perhaps a topically appropriate time
would be now, with the emergence of the ubiquitous Sacajawea
dollar coin.

John Tarnese, sticking firmly to the Oral History of the

Shoshones, said, "The adoption by Clark of Otter Woman's infant daughter caused some in the white world to claim that he wouldn't have adopted the child if it wasn't Sacajawea's. But he did so at her request and that resulted from a simple Sacajawea culture trait. All Shoshoni readily consider immediate adoptions for Shoshoni babies whose parents have died. On the Lewis and Clark journey when Sacajawea quickly adopted Basil, she was acting out that trait the moment she realized his mother, her sister, had died. The whites — when they learned from the journals that Sacajawea was 'totally unselfish,' 'an adoring mother,' 'of a sweet disposition,' 'dedicated and purposeful,' 'resourceful and brave,' and so forth — believed she was truly unique for an Indian girl. Well, that's simply not so, not at all. She was being true to her culture, because Shoshoni girls bore all those traits, even if whites didn't realize it. Does she deserve her acclaim in the white world? Yes. Did she act as the Shoshones would have expected a Shoshoni girl to act under her circumstances on the Lewis and Clark journey? Yes, absolutely. Whites, to this day, don't seem to understand that. But that's why other tribes often raided Shoshoni villages to capture Shoshoni girls, such as Sacajawea and Otter Woman. Please remember, if you will, that in the famous Tom Luttig note that Otter Woman, though mistaken for Sacajawea, was described as being 'the best woman at the fort.' That's another way of saying that she was the 'only Shoshoni woman' at the fort. Whites crave riches and tend to hoard things, creating chasms between the haves and have-nots. But the Plains Indians shared things and that was a definitive culture trait that Sacajawea merely lived up to, to an extent that it amazed the white men on the Lewis and Clark journey. The great Hunkpapa Sioux leader Sitting Bull, you'll recall, had a famous quote after he returned from his 1885 sojourn with the Buffalo Bill Cody Wild West Show. Sitting Bull said, 'The whites have and can make everything but they don't know how to share it.' The white history books also tell that Annie Oakley cried because she observed Sitting Bull giving away all of his money to poor white children in city after city. If that gesture shocked the whites it didn't shock the Plains Indians. If whites would study that famous Sitting Bull quote, they would better understand Sacajawea. And understanding her, they would realize that her warm mothering, her unselfishness, her resourcefulness, her bravery, and so forth, merely revealed Shoshoni traits. As a Shoshoni, I am proud of Sacajawea's uniqueness. But I am just as proud that she was a typical Shoshoni at the time the whites got to know her, on the Lewis and Clark journey."[40]

CHAPTER SIX

In 1935 the U. S. Government saw the need once again to clear up the controversy as to where and when Sacajawea died and where she is buried. John Roberts, the young preacher who officiated at her burial at Fort Washakie in 1884, was an old but very alert man in 1935 and the government wanted his official statement before he died.

On April first, 1935, John Roberts provided the U. S. Government his six-page, official statement on the issue.[41] I enclose at the end of this book an exact copy of that painstaking statement from a man whose intelligence, insight and honesty has never been questioned.

As you can see, John Roberts entitled the first portion of that statement "The Death of Sacajawea." He explained that the Right Reverend John F. Spalding sent him in 1883 to establish the Shoshone and Arapaho mission of the Protestant Episcopal Church.

On his second day on the Wind River Reservation he met Basil, whom he described as "an aged and fine specimen of an Indian."

Roberts was introduced to Basil by Dr. James Irwin, the U. S. Agent in charge of the Shoshone reservation. Basil shortly took him to see his mother, Sacajawea. Roberts said, "She was seated on the ground in a teepee; her hair was gray and she had the appearance of being very old."

Dr. Irwin informed Roberts of Sacajawea's connection to the Lewis and Clark Expedition and Roberts said that Dr. Irwin "seemed to be keenly interested in that fact."

Roberts' official statement also said, "Basil proved to be a very dutiful son to his mother. He cared for her tenderly and had his daughters and other women of the camp see to her every need. She was well provided for."

Like Dr. Irwin before him, Reverend Roberts then entered a period during which conversations with Basil and Sacajawea proved to him that Sacajawea really was the Lewis and Clark heroine. Such conversations were complete with details and mementos that only Sacajawea could possibly have known and possessed.

At the bottom of Page Two Reverend Roberts begins the section that he entitled "The Burial of Sacajawea." He says that America's greatest heroine didn't suffer but simply "passed away suddenly during the night of April ninth, 1884. The burial of Sacajawea took place late in the afternoon on the day on which she died. Those in attendance were her immediate relatives, the Agent and some of the employees. I read over her grave the Burial Service of the Episcopal Church. She sleeps with her face towards the dawn on the sunny slope of the Rocky Mountains. Her grave overlooks the beautiful Wind River Valley."

Reverend Roberts was Basil's good friend. In his official report to the U. S. Government, Roberts said, "Basil, the adopted son and nephew of Sacajawea and in whose camp she lived, died a few years after his mother. He was buried at a place about four miles from the Agency but was subsequently laid to rest beside the grave of Sacajawea, his adopted mother."

Roberts concluded his statement with what white historians should consider sharp insight into how the Shoshones themselves, including Basil, very cautiously viewed Sacajawea's role with the Lewis and Clark Expedition. For example, Roberts recalled that once Bazil had asked for his mother's tent to be pitched close to Dr. Irwin's house, during a time when Basil was going off on a buffalo hunt. While he was gone he wanted Dr. Irwin "to take special care of her, for she has been a great friend of the white people in the early days."

Roberts elaborated on Basil's statement to Dr. Irwin by stating that, "Basil would not have mentioned the fact to Dr. Irwin had he not been anxious for the welfare of his mother during his absence on the hunt." And why was Basil so reticent about Sacajawea's association with Lewis and Clark? Reverend Roberts explained that with these exact words: "Sacajawea, during her life, never boasted of her journey and great service to the whites. In fact, on the other hand, she kept it a secret for if the fact should have been published on her having led the Lewis and Clark Expedition it would have brought nothing but opprobrium and scorn from the members of her tribe."

On the other hand, Roberts maintained that Sacajawea would sometimes discuss intimate details about that journey with special friends, including him.

In this final, official, poignant and revealing statement, the deeply respected man who officiated at Sacajawea's burial counters profusely the conclusions of the anti-Wyoming white historians in regards to the life and death of Sacajawea.

The Reverend John Roberts spent sixty years of his life on the Wind River Reservation in Wyoming. For all those sixty years and till the day he died, the admirable Reverend Roberts knew that it was the real Sacajawea that he buried on the Wind River Reservation on April ninth, 1884. Before he died, Reverend Roberts painstakingly supplied his statement, by request, to the U. S. Government. At the back of this book, I invite you to read that statement from Reverend Roberts, as well as the official statement that Dr. Charles Eastman reported back to the government on his federally funded investigation.

No one, to my knowledge, has ever remotely questioned the intelligence or fairness of either Reverend Roberts or Dr. Eastman.

And, to my mind, the intelligence and fairness of the Shoshoni people themselves, especially in regards to an ancestor, should also not be questioned.

John Tarnese, the Shoshoni expert on the Oral History of the Shoshones, says, "Starting with the Lewis and Clark journey, when she adopted Basil, Sacajawea's decades long attachment to him, so well known to the Shoshones and confirmed by many whites, all alone reveals that she lived a long life in Wyoming, far beyond the 1812 date that some whites, mistaking her for Otter Woman, say she died. If there is controversy concerning Sacajawea, and even

Baptiste, there is none concerning Basil. He was straight as an arrow. He lived a long and fruitful life. For almost eight decades, he knew who his precious, adoptive mother was and there was never a blip in the continuity of all that. Many noted whites on the Wind River Reservation all knew that, too. Basil worshipped his mother all those years. He buried her on April ninth, 1884, at Wind River. The whites who say she died at Fort Manuel in 1812 are stupid. Uh, let me rephrase that, if you will! The whites who say she died at Fort Manuel in 1812 are stupid when it comes to Basil. Ha! Ha! Ha! Otherwise, I presume they are very smart."[42]

CHAPTER SEVEN

All of the anti-Wyoming Sacajawea historians put tremendous stock in an entry that Judge Henry M. Brackenridge put in his journal on April second, 1811, while a passenger aboard a steamboat on the Missouri River. Here is his statement:

> *"We have on board a Frenchman named Charbonneau, with his wife, an Indian of the Snake nation, both of whom accompanied Lewis and Clark to the Pacific and were of great service. The woman, a good creature, of a mild and gentle disposition, is greatly attached to the whites, whose manners and dress she has tried to imitate, but she became sickly and longed to revisit her native country; her husband also, who has spent many years among the Indians, became weary of civilized life.* "[43]

Like John Luttig at Fort Manuel, Judge Brackenridge did not mention Sacajawea by name but Brackenridge did state "both of whom accompanied Lewis and Clark to the Pacific," meaning both Charbonneau and Sacajawea. And that Brackenridge steamboat was heading to Fort Manuel. However, like Luttig, Brackenridge simply confused Otter Woman with Sacajawea.[44] At times, perhaps with Englishmen talking with Canadian/Frenchmen, little details got mixed up and assumptions were made. Regardless, Brackenridge and Luttig, if they wanted to nail something down, should have consulted Shoshoni people, who knew Sacajawea was not on that steamboat.

For example, imagine Brackenridge later looking Basil in the face and saying, "How could you be so stupid, Basil? The woman you have idolized as your mother all these years is not your mother. You see, your mother died at Fort Manuel way back in 1812."

Well, Basil was a powerful man and a true leader among the Shoshoni. A white man confronting him with such talk about Sacajawea would not have been "standing for very long," as my Shoshoni friend John Tarnese and others have repeatedly said.

Four times I have visited Sacajawea's grave and I am not pleased with the upkeep of the rutty field where it is located. Also, there are scant directions to it even though it is just off a prime road leading to and from Yellowstone National Park. Is the state of Wyoming not proud of her or is it merely too meek to challenge the much weaker claim that she is buried in South Dakota?

South Dakota, of course, claims her burial site is just across the North Dakota border on the Standing Rock Reservation, about twenty miles south of Fort Yates.[45]

Both North and South Dakota lavishly explain that Sacajawea tourists should head to Kenel, South Dakota, via Highway 1806 on the west side of the Missouri River between McLaughlin and Herreid, two small South Dakota towns. North Dakota is already booming out information that Sacajawea and the Lewis and Clark Expedition traveled through North Dakota.

Interestingly enough, both North and South Dakota — despite their keen interest in tourism — seem ready to accept Wyoming's much stronger version of where and when Sacajawea died and where she is buried. And both Dakotas openly wonder why Wyoming doesn't rant and rave about its powerful claim to her final resting place.[46]

In an AP article out of Minot, N. D., in the summer of 1999, Rick Collin of the State Historical Society of North Dakota says, "Our purpose is to present the information that's available and then let people decide which Sacajawea is the historically correct one. Deciding which is the true Sacajawea is not our purpose."

I agree with him but, as you can possibly detect, even the two

Dakotas seem mystified as to why Wyoming seems inclined to meekly dismiss its very powerful claims to Sacajawea.

Calvin Grinnel of New Town, North Dakota, a member of the North Dakota Lewis and Clark Bicentennial Advisory Committee, also refuses to remotely discount Wyoming 's claim to Sacajawea's burial place.

Mark Halvorson, curator of collections research for the State Historical Society in North Dakota, merely says, "The important thing of all this is, every generation reevaluates the past."

Halvorson is right and, in regards to Sacajawea, the time for that reevaluation is now.

As I listen to the words and sentiments of John Tarnese, an elderly but very sincere and astute Shoshone, I am reminded of a quote from the famed architect Frank Lloyd Wright. He said that the truth is more important than — and often different from — the facts.

In Sacajawea's case, the "facts" of her "1812" death at Fort Manuel in South Dakota are almost entirely related to those three little notes left behind in 1811, 1812 and 1826 by three white men — Judge Henry Brackenridge, Tom Luttig and William Clark.

The "truth" of Sacajawea's "1884" death at Fort Washakie in Wyoming is based on more pertinent data — namely, her own people, the Shoshones, and two other tribes she associated with for significant periods, the Comanches and Gros Ventres, knew that Sacajawea was very real and very much alive from 1812 till 1884.[47] Furthermore, there are many substantiated "facts" from the white world to corroborate the Shoshones, Comanches and Gros Ventres, "facts" that far outweigh the three little notes left behind by Brackenridge, Luttig and Clark. Stay tuned.

CHAPTER EIGHT

In the first decade of the nineteenth century, Sacajawea became a celebrity in the white world because of the Lewis and Clark Expedition, a status that she neither sought nor anticipated and one that she did not fully understand or desire.[48]

Consider, if you will, how vast, barren and sparsely populated the uncharted West was in 1805 when the Corps of Discovery began its journey. Yet, like finding a needle in a haystack, there were legitimate "sightings" of Sacajawea on that journey, in sharp contrast to the many "false sightings" in the white world that would later mar her historical footsteps.

For example, Sacajawea was astounded to come across her brother, the famous Shoshoni chief named Cameahwait, whom she had not seen since she was eleven-years-old when her village was raided and destroyed by a rival tribe, which killed most of her family and took her as a captive. In his 1814 book entitled "*The Lewis and Clark Expedition,*" Meriwether Lewis described Sacagawea's meeting with her brother in these exact words on Page 334:

> "*Sacajawea was beginning to interpret when in the person of Cameahwait she recognized her brother. She instantly jumped up and ran and embraced him, throwing over him her blanket and weeping profusely; the chief was himself moved.*
>
> *After some conversation between them, she resumed her seat and attempted to interpret for us but her new situation seemed to overpower her and she was frequently interrupted by tears.*
>
> *After the council was finished, Sacajawea learnt that all her family were dead except two brothers, one of whom was*

*absent, and a son of her eldest sister, a small boy, who was
immediately adopted by her.* [9]

That "small boy" — a nephew — that Sacajawea adopted as
her son on August seventeenth, 1805, near the forks of the Jefferson
River was, of course, Basil. He would worship the ground Sacajawea
walked on until he buried her on the Wind River Reservation in
Wyoming on April ninth, 1884.

On the expedition there was another "needle in a haystack"
experience for Sacajawea. She met a childhood friend, a girl named
Rabbit Ear, who had been captured by the rival tribe when
Sacajawea was captured. Meriwether Lewis, in his famous 1814
book, described that euphoric meeting in these exact words:

> "We soon drew near to the camp and just as we ap-
> proached it a woman made her way through the crowd
> towards Sacajawea and, recognizing each other, they em-
> braced with the most tender affection. The meeting of those
> two young women had in it something peculiarly touching,
> not only in the ardent manner in which their feelings were
> expressed, but from the real interest of their situation. They
> had been companions in childhood. They had shared and
> softened the rigours of their captivity, till one of them es-
> caped from the Minnetarees, with scarce hope of ever seeing
> her friend relieved from the hands of her enemies. While
> Sacajawea was renewing among the women the friendships
> of former days, Captain Clark went on and was received by
> the chief."

Those two "needle in a haystack" sightings of Sacajawea,
although extreme long-shots, are historically accurate. Lewis,
Clark and twenty-eight other white men witnessed them and
Sacajawea, her brother and her girlfriend all confirmed them.
Also, all involved had indeed laid eyes on Sacajawea and knew
her intimately.

Lewis and Clark, as they engaged Toussaint Charbonneau, the French-Canadian trapper, as their interpreter in 1804, accepted his wife, Sacajawea, as an additional interpreter. But mostly, it was her gender that initially impressed the two leaders of the expedition the most. "A woman with a party of men is a token of peace," Clark wrote in his journal. And both Lewis and Clark concluded that an Indian woman plus her infant baby would send massive signals to other Indians about the party's peaceful intentions.[50]

Four months into the journey, the expedition needed horses because it had reached the navigable limits of the Missouri River. Lewis contacted a Shoshone tribe and solicited Sacajawea to act as interpreter as he bartered for horses. At the session, Sacajawea's euphoric reunion with her older brother, Chief Cameahwait, also presented her with the option of remaining with her own people or continuing the journey. After obtaining the vital horses from her brother, Sacajawea's sense of adventure led her to commit totally to the entire journey. Shortly, crossing the Bitterroot Mountains, the entire expedition was in dire straits because of snow, hunger and exhaustion. Beyond Shoshoni territory, Sacajawea took the lead in persuading the Nez Perce to take them in. Then Clark wrote in his journal, "She reconciles all the Indians. We, the entire enterprise, would indeed be lost without her."[51]

Adroitly meshing the expedition with the various Indian tribes, Sacajawea not only eased but actually, in all probability, saved the entire enterprise on several occasions.

"Sacajawea definitely had that option to stay with her Shoshoni people or continue the journey," says Shoshoni elder John Tarnese. "If she had chosen to stay with her people, her brother, Chief Cameahwait, clearly would have welcomed her. And neither Clark nor Lewis, and also Charbonneau, would not have been permitted to pressure her. It's important to point out that she may have unwittingly stumbled into the expedition but, early on, she had the clear opportunity to break off from it, and break off from Charbonneau too. The fact she didn't probably saved the expedition and also reveals the adventurous spirit of her Shoshoni character. I believe . . . I have always believed . . . her soul, that adventurous spirit, is pained by the current controversy surrounding her death. You see, there was much more to her life than the Lewis and Clark Expedition. She did not die young, in her twenties, in 1812 at Fort Manuel; she died at about age ninety-six in 1884 at Fort Washakie. Her longevity and her gravesite would forever be important to her, because of her Shoshoni culture. We Shoshones know that. Thus, the white historians who claim she died in 1812 should either prove it or they should shut up. But they can't prove she died in 1812. All they can do is create a controversy. That saddens her soul and that adventurous spirit, too, I'm sure. She was so sweet, so kind and so capable. She sincerely, of her own choice and not by chance or accident, did so much for this country. And this country, with all the honors bestowed upon her, has done a lot for her. But the controversy is frustrating. We, the Shoshones, know when she died, where she died and where she is buried. We are neither liars nor idiots. White historians who say she died seventy-two years before she did can't even convince the best white historians, and certainly don't give the Shoshones any second thoughts. But a few high-profile historians, even though they are wrong, are hurtful to her Shoshoni kin and, most of all, I think, to Sacajawea — that precious soul and that adventurous spirit that I speak of. Yes, early on she had the option to free herself of the rigors of that Lewis and Clark journey. But she persevered. Now, I believe, is it incumbent upon some of us to persevere on her behalf. No one should praise the two years she gave to Lewis and Clark and then discount the final seventy-two years of her life. To her and the Shoshones, that is important too."[5][2]

CHAPTER NINE

Captain Meriwether Lewis never saw his first Shoshoni male until Sunday, August eleventh, 1805. The suspicious warrior reined in his horse and watched anxiously as Lewis moved toward him. Lewis gestured wildly in friendship, offering items to trade, but the Shoshoni turned his horse and dashed into the woods.[53]

But shortly, the Lewis and Clark Expedition established friendly terms with a warrior belonging to the Lemhi Shoshone band of Chief Cameahwait, who happened to be the brother of Sacajawea. This paved the way for the Corps of Discovery to acquire some horses from the Shoshones, who were considered the best horsemen on the Great Plains. Without horses, the expedition quite possibly would have been doomed to failure.[54]

During this period, Chief Cameahwait led a band of northern Shoshones that were constantly threatened by Blackfoot Indians in what is now Idaho. The eastern Shoshones had primarily settled in what is now the Wind River area of Wyoming, with their Comanche cousins. A Comanche band in the 1700s drove the Apaches from the southern plains while the Shoshones, also known as the Snake People, moved toward the headwaters of the Missouri and included the plains of both Wyoming and Montana as prime hunting territories. The Shoshones got horses around 1700 and thus the buffalo-rich plains were much more easily exploited. Very soon, the Shoshones gained a reputation as the best horsemen on the plains and they bartered their own privately bred and tamed horses with other tribes in the Pacific Northwest, including the Crow, the Nez Perces and the Flatheads. Horses also provided warring tribes with another prime excuse to raid the camps of neighbors who had more and better animals.[55]

When Sacajawea was eleven-years-old, in 1801, the Minatarees raided her Shoshoni encampment, killing most of her family and taking her hostage. In 1805, Sacajawea had that famous reunion with her brother, Chief Cameahwait, on the Lewis and Clark Expedition, and Cameahwait told Sacajawea that Atsina raiders had hit his camp just before she arrived.[56]

The Shoshones and Nez Perces were considered the most peaceful of all the Western Indians but they were resourceful and fierce fighters if pushed to the brink. The Utes and Blackfeet often raided Shoshoni villages merely to capture Shoshone women and girls, who were considered prizes for inbreeding purposes. The numerically superior Blackfeet eventually pushed the Shoshones hundreds of miles below the Canadian border, including what was once a Shoshoni stronghold near Eagle Hills, Saskatchewan. In 1781, a pandemic of smallpox hit both the Shoshones and the Blackfeet, killing up to fifty per cent of each tribe. In 1787, a Blackfoot chief name Kutenai Appe led 250 fierce warriors in repeated raids against the Shoshones, according to French trappers who had built trading posts on the Saskatchewan River in the 1730s and 1740s.[57]

By the time Chief Cameahwait met up with Lewis and Clark in 1805, he was complaining that Spanish traders headquartered in Santa Fe, New Mexico, were supplying guns to the Blackfeet, Crows and Arapahoes but not to his Shoshones. Thus, Cameahwait said his people stayed in the mountains most of the time — subsisting on fish, berries and roots — because they didn't have the guns to compete with their enemies for the buffalo on the plains. Trading with whites such as Lewis and Clark was a prime reason Cameahwait was quite friendly to them, a point that Sacajawea made known to the two captains.[58]

In 1835, a trapper named Zenas Leonard wrote: "The Shoshones were once a powerful nation, possessing a glorious hunting ground on the east side of the mountains, but they have been annihilated by the revengeful Blackfeet who, being supplied with firearms, were enabled to defeat all Indian opposition. Their nation (the Snake Indians) has been entirely broken up and scattered throughout the region."[5][9]

Smallpox also intermittently continued to weaken the Shoshones.

But as white American traders became more prominent in the West, the Shoshones secured guns and often battled the powerful Blackfeet, Crows and even the Sioux to standstills. Under strong chiefs such as Mawoma and Washakie, the Shoshones had recaptured much of their lost glory and they were a powerful presence from the Wind River to South Pass and in the vicinity of the North Platte River around Fort Laramie. Chief Washakie was a powerful Shoshone from 1840 until his death in 1900 and he loved whites, and often fought with them against other Indian tribes. The U. S. government richly rewarded Washakie, including parcels of land that became the Wind River Reservation. Bordered on the west by the Wind River Mountains and on the north by the Owl Creek Mountain Range, the Wind River Reservation encompasses about 3,500 square miles in west central Wyoming. The reservation today is home to just over 5,000 members of the Shoshone and Arapahoe tribes, both of whom still maintain strong ties with their cultural and traditional pasts. And for the Shoshones, that includes what they call "the Sacajawea Cemetery," the only place where her proud descendants have ever said she is buried.

The reservation was originally established for the Shoshones in 1863 by the Fort Bridger Treaty and included about 45,000,000 acres in what is now the states of Colorado, Utah, Idaho and Wyoming. But the size diminished in the following century because of a series of new treaties and land purchase agreements. In the spring of 1878, the U. S. military escorted a thousand members of the Arapahoe tribe to the Wind River Reservation, supposedly on a temporary basis. But shortly the government made it permanent although the Shoshones and Arapahoe were ancient enemies. In 1927 Congress permitted the Shoshones to sue for having to share their already diminished reservation with the Arapahoes. In the settlement, the Shoshones got $4.5 million and the Arapahoes acquired an undivided half interest in the reservation. Today, the Shoshones primarily reside on the western side of the reservation with the Arapahoes on the eastern side. Tribal members exist on a friendly and competitive basis with both the Shoshones and Arapahoes having their own governing bodies. The two councils from each tribe come together to act on matters that affect the whole reservation. John Tarnese, my friend and my expert on the Oral/ Traditional History of the Shoshones, was a long-time member of the Shoshoni council. It is a history that reminds him that Sacajawea loved making and selling beadwork on the Wind River Reservation and it is a tradition that continues till this day. Some of the world's best beadwork, readily recognizable by its rose patterns, still emanates from the reservation that Sacajawea called home. Eva McAdams, who managed the Warm Valley Arts and Crafts Center at Fort Washakie for many years, says, "Sacajawea and the Shoshones considered the rose the world's most beautiful flower. That's why they selected it for beading. It symbolized goodness and love. Yes, till her death in 1884, Sacajawea tended to her roses and incorporated rose patterns in her beadwork. She set the standard in beading that is still taught to this day at Wind River. When I think of her I think that she was as sweet and as precious as the rose flowers that she loved so much."

Chief Washakie led the Shoshones for over sixty years, from 1840 until his death on February twenty-first, 1900. It is believed he was born in 1798 or 1799, which would mean he lived in three centuries. He was given a full military funeral and buried in the old military cemetery at Fort Washakie, right across a dirt road from where Sacajawea had been buried in 1884. Chief Washakie's casket was carried on a caisson, volleys were fired over his grave and taps sounded by an army bugler. The inscription over his tomb reads: "Always loyal to the government and to his white brothers." Thus, the two most famous Shoshones — Sacajawea and Chief Washakie — shared much in common, including longevity and a deep-rooted love for whites. From about 1790 until 1884, Sacajawea was a part of that Shoshoni world, except for the two years she devoted to the Lewis and Clark Expedition and the time she sub-sequently spent in the St. Louis area under the sponsorship of William Clark.

In the Shoshoni culture, females, from an early age, bonded with other females more tightly than in other cultures. This was out of necessity as much as anything else and was reflected in the fact that girls and women worked closely together in such things as procuring and preserving foodstuffs as well as crafting bedding and clothing.

Shoshoni women, to this day, are among the best in the world at fashioning such trinkets as beads and creating beautiful designs out of cloth and hides, often stressing a specific theme built around their love for that particular flower — the rose. In the 1850s and 1860s, prior to settling on the Wind River Reservation, Sacajawea lived in or near white settlements so she would have a market for beads and trinkets that she herself fashioned.[60]

When it came to medical needs, women characteristically took great care of other women, especially in the birthing and rearing of Shoshoni babies. At the same time, Shoshoni females were taught to revere men and to accept even their barbaric traits. Thus, Sacajawea, as an eleven-year-old girl, was not too bent out of shape when a rival tribe mauled her village and took her captive. Such stoicism can be equated to a child born and reared on a small island surrounded by alligators; from the outset, the child takes the alligators in stride.[61]

Shoshoni women on the plains earned a solid reputation for being pretty, dignified, disciplined, reserved and stoic but also quite skilled and dedicated. The white men on the Lewis and Clark Expedition very readily detected all of these characteristics in their acute observations of Sacajawea. For example, time and again the diary-keepers marveled over the fact that Sacajawea, regardless of the dire hardships and the many deprivations, never once com-plained about anything — except that one time when she let Wil-liam Clark know she deserved to be taken to the shore of the Pa-cific Ocean so she could see the "monstrous fish" the other men had told her about.[62]

So, on the Voyage of Discovery, Sacajawea was very much a Shoshoni. But she was also special, very special. For example, once during a period of hunger, the meat-loving men took to eating dog meat. However, Sacajawea firmly told William Clark, "I no eat dog!" And she never did. She enchanted the men, especially William Clark, with her signature style of dedication, understatement and discretion.

The perceptive and often highly critical Meriwether Lewis noted how "cultured" Sacajawea was, even compared to white women that he had known. She dressed in soft, discreet, buckskin clothing while Lewis pointedly took cognizance that other Indian women they came upon were often attired in "hard leather" that left little to the imagination when they "bent over."[63]

Sexually, Sacajawea was not God's little angel although most historians have sanitized the Lewis and Clark Expedition in that regard. The oral history of the Shoshones registers the fact that Sacajawea, during the course of the expedition, stepped outside her "marriage" to the rogue Charbonneau and had sex with three other members of the troupe — Meriwether Lewis, William Clark and Clark's Negro servant York. Ironically, to prevent such shenanigans, Lewis and Clark made it a point, at the outset of the journey, to insist on a marriage ceremony to officially link Sacajawea and Charbonneau as man and wife in white eyes. There is enough in the diaries and journals to convince many historians that Sacajawea was briefly engaged in sexual activity with both Lewis and Clark and Shoshoni oral histories bear this out. Also, Shoshoni oral history reveals the fact that the teenage Sacajawea "tried" York, Clark's Negro servant.[64] All along the way, Indian women who encountered the expedition were verily fascinated with York and the "black paint that would not rub off his skin." So, as she would admit years later when she returned to the Shoshoni world, it is, perhaps, understandable that Sacajawea would "try" York.[65]

While Sacajawea was a little bit promiscuous, she was not at all reckless. Clark noted that "she, in all aspects, set the standard for cleanliness." And Clark would know. Twice on the journey, she became quite ill and both times Clark ascribed her troubles merely to severe "problems with her monthly cycles" and he successfully treated her illness accordingly.[66]

Apart from Sacajawea, syphilis reared its ugly head during the Lewis and Clark Expedition as any unsanitized account will attest.

By September nineteenth, 1805, many of the men were suffering from skin lesions, a secondary symptom of syphilis. In August of 1805 Lewis led a group of men over the Continental Divide, where they encountered a friendly band of Shoshone in Idaho. On August thirteenth, Lewis and his men relished an all-night celebration with Shoshoni women. Five days later, Lewis wrote in his journal that he "viewed with regret the many hours I have spent in indolence."[67]

Some Shoshoni chiefs, anxious to trade with the whites, had a unique way of showing their friendship — by providing the white men some delectable young Shoshoni women. Lewis registered that fact in his diary with these words: "I cannot prevent sexual relations between our white men and such Indian women because for these young men some months of abstinence have made them very polite to these tawny damsels."

Well, Lewis himself fell victim to the enticement. In fact, when Lewis shot himself to death in a Tennessee cabin on October eleventh, 1809, historians generally agree it was because of the ravages of syphilis that he contracted while on the Journey of Discovery. Two powerful men, Thomas Jefferson and William Clark, would later admit that the chronically depressed Lewis did indeed commit suicide. However, both Jefferson and Clark did their best to steer historians away from the fact that Lewis, still in his mid-thirties, had become ill and mentally deranged from the venereal disease that, for Lewis and others, was a legacy of the famed expedition.

Clark's closeness to Sacajawea may have saved him from Lewis' fate because there is some evidence to indicate, in Clark's mention of her "cleanliness," that she forewarned him about the dangers of syphilis along the way. Clark even makes reference to "the sex debt of action" he owed her when his journal mentioned the fact that he had saved the lives of Sacajawea and her infant Pomp when they otherwise would "surely have drowned" in a raging torrent.[68]

To briefly "unsanitize" the Lewis and Clark Expedition in regards to syphilis, merely illustrates that the teenage Sacajawea was an astute, independent and imperfect soul, not irrevocably tied to her Shoshoni culture or to the powers of the white world that she had stepped into.

CHAPTER TEN

While some may consider it benign, I believe it is history's duty to follow Sacajawea's life all the way to 1884, not just to 1812.

The architects of the 1812 theory must be challenged. To do so, the oral history of the Shoshones, her own people, must take precedence over three little notes — Luttig's, Brackenridge's and Clark's — although that oral history, of a certainty, should be corroborated against written words from the whites whenever possible.

If whites control the newspapers and the rest of the media, as well as the history books, they should be particularly scrupulous when it comes to getting their facts straight concerning an indigenous culture that may be foreign to them.

First and foremost, consider the culture of the Shoshones. They were not sophisticated liars and, compared to the white world, they had no comprehension of concocting meaningful lies. Also, in Sacajawea's case, the Shoshones wanted to minimize, not maximize, her involvement with the very white Lewis and Clark Expedition, and thus they were devoid of motives to lie about Sacajawea's true identity. They didn't, for example, envision making piles of money by writing books about her or utilizing her celebritism in the white world to market a realm of false goods to the whites. To the Shoshones, giving away material goods was better than receiving them, a trait that Sacajawea took with her on the Lewis and Clark Expedition.[69]

Refurbished, I hope, with that backdrop, let's now examine Sacajawea's life in two precise, capsule forms — from birth till 1812, including the 1805-06 Voyage of Discovery; and 1812 to 1884, when she also led a meaningful and dignified life.

The Shoshones say Sacajawea was born in the summertime, probably in the year of 1790, among the Lemhi Shoshones in the region that is now central Idaho and western Montana.

At about age eleven, she was kidnapped by warriors of the Gros Ventre Indians, who took her back to their village on the upper Missouri in North Dakota. She was later traded to the Minataree Indians and lived in a village near where the Knife River slices into the Missouri River. Then she was purchased in 1803 by the French-Canadian trader Toussaint Charbonneau, who took her as one of his "wives."[70]

Sacajawea and Charbonneau — on November eleventh, 1804 — met up with the Lewis and Clark Expedition. She was believed to be fourteen-years-old and known to be very pregnant. Charbonneau hired on as a guide and told Lewis and Clark he wanted Sacajawea to stay with him. Reluctantly, they agreed. Then they insisted Charbonneau marry Sacajawea in a white man's ceremony, specifically to register her status with the other men in the troupe. Soon, after orchestrating the wedding, Lewis and Clark both were instrumental in helping Sacajawea through the difficult task of delivering her first baby. As the severity of the pain mounted, Lewis and Clark concocted a potion — rattlesnake rattles smashed into a powder and then boiled into a liquid. Sacajawea, within ten minutes of drinking the potion, gave birth to a son, whom she named Baptiste. William Clark nicknamed the infant Pomp — meaning "first born" in Shoshoni— and that's what Sacajawea called him. William Clark, from the outset, also referred to Pomp as "my son" and "my boy."

Clark's intimacy with Sacajawea during the birthing process left an indelible mark on him. He was enthralled with her looks as well as her "sharp wits and sweet disposition." And he took note of her "tender, instinctive mothering."

The Lewis and Clark Expedition — which included Sacajawea, Pomp and Charbonneau — left Fort Mandan on April seventh, 1805.[71]

Prior to the birth, Sacajawea had fashioned a cradleboard so her baby could be strapped to her back. Little did she know that the image of her with the papoose in the cradleboard would emerge as one of the most cherished and honored images in what was to become the greatest, richest and most powerful country in the world — America.

While still a teenager — and one who had spent five years as a captured Indian girl, then was sold as a slave to a rogue — she was destined to carve out a legend that would inspire more memorials to her than to any other female in American history.

On May twenty-sixth, 1805, the expedition caught its first view of the Rocky Mountains.

It didn't take long for Lewis and Clark to determine that the invidious Charbonneau was "mostly useless" but the teenage Sacajawea, with a baby upon her back, was "invaluable." The incredibly rough terrain did not intimidate her and, moreover, she, unlike Charbonneau, took an earnest interest in the overall success of the mission, which she understood to be "a mapping of a route to the Great Water — the Pacific Ocean."[7 2]

If she was not the quintessential, legendary "guide" each step of the way, she was readily consulted by the two skilled map-makers, Lewis and Clark, about specific routes and the lay of the land. At times, she most certainly did stand on rocky ledges, with her papoose on her back, and point out features of the landscape and offer opinions on what lay ahead. Her advice, regarding the terrain and living off the land, was both solicited and trusted. And early on, both Lewis and Clark marveled over the fact that Sacajawea was not only quite "astute and dedicated" but also, in the words of Meriwether Lewis, "the non-complainer of the group, and she with the baby to tend to."

On July twenty-fifth, 1805, they camped on the Three Forks of the Missouri River. By now, Lewis and Clark considered Sacajawea a crucial member of the entourage, and Charbonneau was the "tag-along." She spoke choppy English but good French and the mostly inept and self-possessed Charbonneau was utilized to sometimes translate her French into English. Three other members of the troupe — George Drouillard, Pierre Cruzatte and Francois Labiche — were all sons of French-Canadian fathers and Indian mothers and they, too, were sometimes used to help Sacajawea translate. Lewis and Clark also learned to interpret much of Sacajawea's sign language. For example, when she tapped her heart and then pointed out new terrain, that meant she was in familiar territory. And when she sucked her fingers, that meant she was among her own people, or literally "people of the same blanket."[73]

In the summer of 1805, the expedition came across territory that Sacajawea recognized and she indeed guided Lewis and Clark through it, offering valuable insight to the map-makers. Once again displaying her keen interest in the success of the mission, Sacajawea herself was the one who rescued precious records, medicine and mapping equipment when a wobbly boat tumbled them into dangerous waters. By the time the diaries and journals registered that Sacajawea saved the valuable supplies, the teenage girl with the papoose had become the superstar of the vital, arduous and dangerous mission. Lewis dubbed her "indispensable" and Clark, of course, was awestruck.[74]

On August seventeenth, 1805, the expedition met up with the tribe of Sacajawea's father, and the chief was now her brother Cameahwait. He told her that all of her family was dead except for him, another brother and a nephew. Sacajawea adopted that nephew and named him Basil.

Sacajawea had the option of staying with her people, Cameahwait's tribe. Charbonneau, who was more comfortable around Indians than whites, was agreeable. But the spirited Sacajawea was now concerned with helping and being a part of the expedition that was determined to reach the Pacific Ocean. She opted to stay with the expedition, keeping her unweaned papoose Pomp with her but leaving the adopted Basil with Cameahwait, vowing to reclaim him on the return voyage.[75]

On August thirtieth, 1805, the expedition resumed its journey, with Sacajawea and Pomp its most salient adornments.

Into the Rocky Mountain winter of 1805, Sacajawea, more

then once, saved the expedition — from hunger, from hostile Indians that she took it upon herself to communicate with, and from the scarcity of horses. When starvation threatened, it was Sacajawea who located and procured edible food; when Indians targeted the white men's supplies or angrily resented the intrusion, it was Sacajawea who mellowed them; and when horses were required to continue the journey overland, it was Sacajawea who negotiated trades with the Indians.[76]

In November of 1805, the expedition reached the Pacific Ocean and built a fort where the Lewis and Clark River now enters the Columbia River. All along the way, Sacajawea had mesmerized Lewis and Clark with her "sweet disposition." Not once had she complained about anything and not once had she asked for anything special, although she was the one nursing a baby.

However, at the fort she did finally register a little complaint and coyly asked her dear friend William Clark for something. She did so with those tender, loving words that are recorded for history: "I have come so far with us and . . . I find it hard that you do not take me to the shore to see the Great Water and the monstrous fish that others have told me about."

On January sixth, 1806, Sacajawea was taken to the shore where she not only saw the Great Water — the Pacific Ocean — but also saw whales, including one that had beached itself on shore.[77]

The expedition stayed on the edge of the Pacific Ocean until March twenty-third, 1806, which was the date the journey back east began. Sacajawea had no idea she was heading back toward legendary acclaim in the white world.

She kept that promise to her brother, Chief Cameahwait, and reclaimed her adopted son, Basil. He would emerge, right to her dying day decades later, as her closest relative and most ardent friend.

On August sixteenth, 1806, the expedition reached Fort Mandan, only to find it destroyed by fire. It was here that Sacajawea and Charbonneau left the expedition because Charbonneau said he "preferred Indians to civilization." William Clark, not wanting to be separated from Sacajawea or "my son" Pomp, begged them not to leave but he failed. However, he secured a promise from Sacajawea that they would meet again — in St. Louis.

In August of 1807, Sacajawea and her sons — Baptiste and Basil — reunited with William Clark in St. Louis. By now, the Lewis and Clark Expedition was engraved on the contemporary and historical mind of America. And Sacajawea was famous in the white world because of the now published diaries and journals that registered her omnipotent value to the mission. Images of the dedicated Indian girl with the "sweet disposition," and with the papoose on her back, began to take hold. Paintings, statues and memorials of Sacajawea and Pomp began laying a foundation for the maternal legend that would forever remain the most lasting image of the vital, historical mission.[78]

Fame didn't concern Sacajawea but William Clark and the welfare of her two sons did. She was still with William Clark in St. Louis in 1812 when they got word that Otter Woman, one of Charbonneau's other "wives," had died of the fever at Fort Manuel.

Sacajawea's emerging independence, and her disgust over Charbonneau's flaunting his other "wives," had created breaks and rifts in her relationship with the roving French-Canadian, who was about thirty-two years her senior.

Otter Woman had been the only one of Charbonneau's "other wives" that Sacajawea liked. She made that known to William Clark. When they learned that Otter Woman had left behind an infant daughter named Lizette at Fort Manuel, William Clark ended up adopting the baby girl, not because of Otter Woman but to appease Sacajawea, who influenced him greatly.[79]

Sacajawea maintained a close relationship with William Clark in and around St. Louis until 1820. During this period, Clark made sure that Pomp and Basil were taken care of and educated, especially "my son" Pomp.

Charbonneau intermittently reemerged in Sacajawea's life, but it was always stormy because she was no longer a captured and purchased little Indian girl. A brass Charbonneau had two other

Indian "wives" when he showed up back in St. Louis in 1820. Sacajawea, making a faint to get back to her Indian world, actually left St. Louis once with Charbonneau and his other two "wives" heading in a southwesterly direction. On that occasion, she left both Pomp and Basil, who were then teenagers, in Clark's care, at a convent school, which she heartily approved of. Soon, a no longer reticent Sacajawea had a major quarrel with Charbonneau's jealous "wife" named Eagle, and he beat her, although Sacajawea fought back furiously. She then left him, never to see him again.

On her own, Sacajawea returned to St. Louis to check on her sons and to see William Clark. They determined that Pomp, who had taken to the white man's ways, had best remain with Clark but that Basil, who cherished his adopted mother with a passion, would never embrace anything but her Shoshoni culture.

It was on that return to St. Louis that Sacajawea informed William Clark that fame in the white world was of no interest to her. She longed to return, as anonymously as possible, back to the world that had given birth to her — the world of the Plains Indians, her comfort zone. William Clark listened and, because he loved her, he relented.

With the aide of William Clark, her most fervent admirer in the white world, Sacajawea was turned loose, like a feral colt that had been tamed but had never lost that instinctive desire to return to the wild.

It is believed by Shoshoni oral historians that the last time Sacajawea laid eyes on William Clark was the spring of 1821. That parting, a key link in the Sacajawea chain, left "tears marring the eyes of both Clark and Sacajawea," according to that family history passed down to generations of Shoshones. They maintain that Sacajawea requested that she and Clark never meet again, because she only had it in her to say one "final good-bye" to him.

In the years from 1821 till his death in 1838, William Clark would amass fortunes as well as high government offices. He would marry a lady named Julia Hancock on January fifth, 1808, in Fincastle, Virginia, but he never forgot Sacajawea. He understood her desire to live out the remainder of her life with her people, the Plains Indians who would never hound her about her Lewis and Clark fame.[80]

The historians who claim Sacajawea died at Fort Manuel in 1812 put untold emphasis on William Clark's 1826 notation: "Se car ja we ar: Dead." Was he misinformed or did he lie? The Shoshones believe he merely lied, to keep his pact with Sacajawea and to provide the subterfuge she had requested. He knew that "death" would be the greatest cover for Sacajawea from the "hounding" noses of newspapers and historians. And he knew that the "feral colt," which had done so much for America, deserved whatever she wanted, and most of all she wanted to live out her life as quietly as possible on the Great Plains.

Thus, the last great gift William Clark bestowed on her was the gift of freedom and in 1826 he merely tied another ribbon around it.

The Sacajawea that merged back into the world of the Plains Indians wore the gold-rimmed Jefferson Medal around her neck, and she wore it proudly.[81] Historians who claim that Sacajawea died at Fort Manuel in 1812 simply cannot explain away the fact that many Indians and many whites saw Sacajawea wearing that Jefferson Medal many decades beyond 1812. That pertinent medal, over the years, induced Sacajawea to relate unpublished associations with Lewis and Clark that only she could have possibly experienced. Furthermore, although she rarely tried to embellish her involvement with Lewis and Clark, there are undeniable instances that flare up between 1812 and 1884 when Sacajawea displayed and discussed the medal — both to Indians and many, many whites.[82]

Dr. James Irwin, the U. S. Agent in charge of the Shoshones on the Wind River Reservation, and Sarah Irwin are prime examples of whites that knew Sacajawea intimately and knew, beyond doubt, that she was the Lewis and Clark heroine.

Dr. Irwin made it a point to state exactly how many times — a total of "three" — that he actually held Sacajawea's Jefferson

Medal in his "own two hands." Sarah, on the other hand, held it "many times" in discussions with Sacajawea. At such times, among trusted friends, Sacajawea would often relate anecdotes about the Lewis and Clark Expedition that no one else could have done. Apart from special white friends, Sacajawea's own people, the Shoshones, were abundantly aware of that Jefferson Medal and Sacajawea's everlasting love of it. To many whites and to many Shoshones, Sacajawea loved to point out the gold rim around the edges of her prized Jefferson Medal.[83]

I hereby challenge historians such as Steven Ambrose, Ken Burns and T. A. Larson — all of whom claim Sacajawea died at Fort Manuel in 1812 — to explain away her decades-long attachment to the Jefferson Medal, an attachment well known to the Shoshones and to many whites.

Also, when she parted from William Clark, Sacajawea carried a sack — a brown one — that contained other mementos of her days with Lewis and Clark. The Shoshones say that sack was like "an appendage" to Sacajawea "right to her end in 1884." It is known by corroboration in the white world — including key Wind River residents who knew Sacajawea well, such as James and Sarah Irwin and Agricultural Minister F. G. Burnett — that Sacajawea's sack contained such things as personal letters and official documents addressed to her and unmistakably signed by Meriwether Lewis and William Clark, both of whom had well-known signatures.[84]

Later, Sacajawea's precious sack contained a letter addressed to her and signed, "In admiration, Brigham Young." He, of course, was the great leader who led his Mormons into the valley of the Great Salt Lake on July twenty-fourth, 1847. He, too, had a legendary and verified signature.

Mormon missionaries became closer to the Plains Indians than any other whites, by far. One of them was a Mormon lady the Shoshones knew as "Bessie Smith." Bessie was an intimate of Sacajawea's at "three different encampments" and she was familiar with the Jefferson Medal and the contents of the brown sack.

Sacajawea reminisced with Bessie about her days with the Lewis and Clark Expedition. Once, Sacajawea told Bessie about "the fish story." William Clark, on the journey, got so frustrated about not being able to catch a trout for supper that he hurled his pole into the unyielding water. Sacajawea raced down the banks of the stream, fetched a stick and retrieved the pole. She then tossed the string back into the water and almost instantly caught a big trout, to Clark's astonishment. At supper, Clark ventured the thought that he would have caught the big trout if he had been "just a bit more patient." But Sacajawea playfully admonished him with these words: "No you would not have, because you were mad at the fish and I was not."

It was through Bessie Smith, who was well versed both in the Sacajawea legend and the history of the Lewis and Clark Expedition, that such unpublished anecdotes as the "fish story" were later confirmed by William Clark. Also, Bessie was well aware of the letter from her leader, Brigham Young, that ended up in Sacajawea's brown sack. Bessie confirmed the authenticity of that letter.[85]

Thus, not only did her own people, the Shoshones, well know that Sacajawea lived until 1884, but so did many reliable and richly informed whites. Yet, noted historians still use three little, explainable notes from white men — Luttig, Brackenridge and Clark — to discredit the Shoshoni people as well as many whites who knew her intimately from the years 1812 to 1884. And beyond those three notes, the anti-Wyoming historians have no credible evidence whatsoever that Sacajawea died in 1812 at Fort Manuel.

In the concluding chapters I will continue to show you that Sacajawea's own family, her own tribe and many, many more well-positioned whites knew she died in Wyoming in 1884.

CHAPTER ELEVEN

The Wyoming region that Sacajawea called home for most of her life became known to whites early in the nineteenth century. The gap through the Rockies at South Pass was discovered in 1812. Jedemiah Smith journeyed westward beyond the Continental Divide in 1824 and his path became a familiar route of travel for fur traders. Captain Benjamin Bonneville led a team that made great geographical discoveries in the region in 1833. John C. Fremont's 1842 explorations of the Wind River Range greatly heightened interest in the area that would become Wyoming Territory in 1876 and the State of Wyoming in 1890.[86]

John Colter, a Virginian born in 1775, joined the Lewis and Clark Expedition in October, 1803, at Louisville, Kentucky, and later crossed the Continent with them. He returned as far as the Mandan Indian village at the mouth of the Knife River in North Dakota. He left the expedition in August, 1806, and in the summer and fall of 1807 led the Manuel Lisa party to the mouth of the Bighorn River in the region that would become Montana. Lisa then sent Colter alone on a mission to the Crow Indians, which took him across the Wind River and Teton Range in Wyoming into what is now Yellowstone National Park, making Colter the first white man to see the area. In 1808 Colter was severely wounded in a battle between Crow and Blackfeet Indians at the Three Forks of the Missouri River in Montana. In the winter of 1809—1810, Colter led another expedition in the Three Forks area under assignment by the St. Louis Missouri Fur Company under Pierre Menard and Andrew Henry. The group was attacked by hostile Indians and Colter was again wounded. He then retired to a farm near Dundee, Missouri, where he died in 1813.[87]

Beginning in 1862, the U. S. Government offered free land to people who would move out West, meaning west of the Mississippi. This was called "homesteading" and they had to plant a crop and build a house and settle in before they could really own the land. But as late as 1877, the whites were still searching for paths through the Rockies, something the Indians had already discovered, such as the Washakie Trail that crossed the Continental Divide at an elevation of 11,600 feet near the confluence of the East Fork and Little Wind rivers.

Despite the exploits of the 1805-06 Lewis and Clark Expedition, Sacajawea was in her sixties before whites began to settle in her chosen area of Wyoming. The first whites that ventured to Wyoming with the intention of settling down were a group of fifty-five Mormons who arrived in November, 1853. Prior to that, the discovery of gold in California in 1848 had merely influenced Easterners to cross the Wyoming mountains and plains, although most opted for sea passage via Cape Horn to avoid what they still believed were the inhospitable and insurmountable Rocky Mountain barriers. Only the westward push of the Union Pacific Railroad created Wyoming towns, such as Cheyenne in 1867 and Laramie in 1868. There were less than 500 whites in Wyoming in 1860 and less than 10,000 in 1870. Thus the Indians still controlled the region, although the Sand Creek Massacre in 1864 and the Washita Massacre in 1868 reminded them that the whites were bent on the annihilation of the native inhabitants. Victory by the Sioux in the Red Cloud War of the late 1860s pushed back the inevitable a few years. But white reaction to the Sitting Bull-orchestrated victory at the Little Bighorn on June twenty-fifth, 1876, changed things forever, beginning the last gasps of the Plains Indians dominance over a region the more powerful whites finally coveted.[88]

For the last four-and-a-half decades of Sacajawea's life, her Shoshoni people were led by Chief Washakie. As noted earlier, he was fiercely loyal to his people and, like Sacajawea, a lover of whites.

He was visited on the Wind River Reservation by President Chester Arthur and he was given a U. S. military funeral because he and his braves fought and scouted for generals such as George Crook against other Indians, especially the Sioux.

A strict disciplinarian, Chief Washakie had an iron-fisted rule that permitted his Shoshones only one warning. Once, his mother-in-law moved a tent to an area that displeased him, so he had it moved back to its original site and warned her not to move it again. She did, while he was away hunting. When he returned, he personally shot her for disobeying him. Another time, four Shoshoni men got drunk and abused their families. They were warned not to do it again but they did and Chief Washakie, following his no-second-warning dictum to the letter, had them shot.

Chief Washakie admired Sacajawea and praised her service to the Lewis and Clark Expedition although, like all of his people, he was not inclined to make a big deal out of it.[89]

Upon her arrival to the Chief Washakie-dominated Wind River Reservation, Sacajawea was accompanied by her son Basil, his wife and their five children — Maggie, Nancy, Ellen, Andrew and Edrocke. Her renown earned them special consideration. They were given a very comfortable house within a few feet of the Agency headquarters and soon the John Burns' store was erected very close to it. It was in this special house on the Wind River Reservation that Sacajawea died. Basil and his daughter Maggie witnessed her peaceful death in the early morning of April ninth, 1884.[90]

CHAPTER TWELVE

I am, frankly, taken aback by the anti-Sacajawea venom that dots our landscape; further, I ascribe this phenomenon as a primary reason that her death on April ninth, 1884, on the Wind River Reservation is not accepted by historical revisionists.

For example, after Sacajawea was selected as the image on the upcoming Golden Dollar Coin that will, with much fanfare, be issued publicly in March of the year 2000, Kristine Holmgren, on August sixth, 1998, wrote a scathing article in the Minneapolis Star Tribune under the banner headline, "Choice of Sacajawea For New Dollar Coin Shortchanges America."

On June twenty-third, 1998, Kim Ode wrote in the Minneapolis Star Tribune a blistering, egregious article entitled, "Sacajawea As Liberty Is Just History Gone Bad."

On December twenty-third, 1998, Ruth Padawer wrote in The Record (Bergen County, NJ) a hateful article entitled, "Feminists Question Mint's Maternal Instincts."

On January seventh, 1999, in a publication called "University Wire," Jessica Weeks wrote a demeaning article entitled, "U. S. Doesn't Coin Good Idea With Baby."

The obvious incongruity of such unfair swipes at Sacajawea, I believe, cannot be simply dismissed merely because they are ridiculous, not with such scholarly forums spitting it out. She is not some weird anachronism; with focused clarity she led a decent, meaningful life.

In regards to Sacajawea, probably the third most influential Wyoming historian — behind Dr. Grace Hebard and Dr. T. A. Larson — is Blanche Schroer. In her famous essay entitled "Sacajawea: The Legend and the Truth" Schroer wrote, on Page thirty-nine, these exact words: "However, Sacajawea was not a guide as the subtitle of Dr. Hebard's book and a Daughters of the American Revolution memorial in her honor state. Her only real contribution in this area came on the single occasion, on the return trip, when she suggested the route over the Bozeman Trail. Even this information was not vital to the expedition's success. Art work and writings which depict Sacajawea leading the two geniuses of geography, Captains Lewis and Clark, westward across the land can only be termed as laughable."[9] [1]

Well, in my opinion, what is really "laughable" are the multitude of anti-Sacajawea feminists and revisionists. Therefore, if I appear somewhat aggressive in my defense of Sacajawea please understand its necessity. At the moment, it seems, the anti-Sacajawea people are particularly stirred up because of that latest broadside — the upcoming Golden Dollar Coin — that merely enhances the legend of the Indian girl that already is the most memorialized female in American history.

What, may I ask, is there about Sacajawea not to like? Yes, she was an Indian, and proud of it. She was also unbiased, modest, caring, resourceful, intelligent, pretty, productive and, perhaps most of all, the consummate mother. She rode life's waves and nuances as well as anyone ever rode them — without complaints or requests for any special favors. Her presence clarified the character of one of America's greatest adventures—- the Lewis and Clark Expedition. Fame crashed down upon Sacajawea although she did not seek it out and neither she nor her people, the Shoshones, ever tried to exploit it. Instead, as gracefully as possible, she tried to walk away from it.

Study, if you will, the image of Sacajawea on the year 2000 Golden Dollar Coin, a caricature beautifully sculptured by the great Glenna Goodacre. Sacajawea, with her papoose sleeping peacefully in his cradleboard, is looking back over her right shoulder, as if to move away from, not toward, the glory and the criticism shadowing her trail.

She surely never intentionally sought out fame, glory or riches.

That wasn't her nature, and Glenna Goodacre captures the essence of Sacajawea's character in her magnificent sculpture.

The feminists and the revisionists who dislike Sacajawea must understand that those who love her will not stand idly by while she is maligned, and we believe that to subtract seventy-two years of her life, without sufficient proof, is to malign her.

All the anti-Sacajawea books, articles and speeches combined cannot dent the image that Glenna Goodacre and millions of others will always share of the Indian girl that carved out two rather significant niches in her very "non-laughable" life — America's greatest heroine and America's greatest role model.

In 1902, Eva Emery Dye wrote a great book entitled "The Conquest" so the Twentieth Century would "rediscover our Indian girl, Sacajawea."

In 1904, Rollin Bond, the top bandleader in New York City, wrote a beautiful intermezzo classic entitled "Sacajawea."

In 1905, Henry Altman created a hauntingly beautiful statue depicting Sacajawea astride an Indian pony.

In 1905, a lady named Alice Cooper designed a gorgeous statue with the inscription, "For the women of the United States in memory of Sacajawea." It adorns the Lakeview Terrace in Portland, Oregon.

In 1906, Edward Samuel Paxson produced an oil painting of Sacajawea that still graces the library at the University of Montana.

In 1909, H. E. Wadsworth and T. H. Burke constructed a splendid concrete shaft with an imbedded bronze tablet for Sacajawea's gravesite headstone on the Wind River Reservation.

In 1910, Cyrus Edwin Dallin designed a realistic statue of Sacajawea pointing the way for Lewis and Clark.

In 1910, Leonard Crunelle created a lovely bronze statue of Sacajawea. It was dedicated to the school children of South Dakota and is still located on the capital grounds at Bismarck.

In 1914, the Montana Daughters of the American Revolution placed a granite boulder with a brass tablet "In Patriotic Memory of Sacajawea" near the three forks of the Missouri.

In 1914, a boulder with a bronze tablet was dedicated to Sacajawea at Armstead, Montana, by the Montana Daughters of the American Revolution. This was the spot where Sacajawea reunited with her brother, Chief Cameahwait, on August seventeenth, 1805.

In 1915, Laura Tolman Scott wrote a drama entitled "Sacajawea" under the sponsorship of the Montana Daughters of the American Revolution. It headlined a lavish pageant staged in the Valley of the Beaverhead River, at the spot where Sacajawea rediscovered her Shoshoni people during the Lewis and Clark Expedition.

In 1918, Charles Marion Russell painted a huge, gorgeous mural depicting Sacajawea's 1805 meeting with her brother. It is now at the back of the speaker's desk in the House of Representatives in Helena, Montana.

In 1919, the U. S. Government named a battleship "Wyoming" and the governor of Wyoming, Joseph M. Carey, requested that its emblem bear a silver likeness of Sacajawea, the Indian girl that Governor Carey believed best symbolized his proud state.

In 1920, the scenic lake in Longview, Washington, was named Lake Sacajawea.

In 1925, Tullius P. Dunlap's striking painting entitled "The Shoshones and Sacajawea" was dedicated to Beaverhead Valley, Montana.

In 1927, an airplane named "The Spirit of Sacajawea" made its initial flight over the ancient hunting grounds of the Shoshones in the state of Wyoming.

In 1930, a peak 13,737 feet high located on the Continental Divide was officially named Mount Sacajawea, at the urging of U. S. Forest Ranger Alfred G. Clayton of Wyoming. It's located in the Wind River range.

In 1931, a bronze tablet was placed on the outer wall of the Bishop Randall Chapel at Fort Washakie, Wyoming, to signify the fact that "four of Sacajawea's grandchildren" were baptized at that spot back on August nineteenth of 1873.

In 1932, Evangeline Close and William Lester teamed to write a cantata entitled "Sacajawea, A Legend" and it remains a staple of the Toledo (Ohio) Choral Society.

In 1932, two granite monuments were placed in the Shoshone Indian Cemetery at Fort Washakie, Wyoming, to honor Basil, the beloved adopted son of Sacajawea, and Barbara Meyers, a daughter of Baptiste and granddaughter of Sacajawea.

In 1932, the Daughters of the American Revolution and the U. S. Forest Service honored the states of Montana and Idaho with the Interstate Sacajawea National Monument. It is located at Lemhi Pass 7,500 feet high on the Continental Divide at the boundary between Montana and Idaho. That is the spot where Sacajawea, in August of 1805, personally guided the Lewis and Clark Expedition over a very treacherous and narrow path.

These are just a few of the many honors that have come to Sacajawea and made her the most memorialized female in American history; and the honors will keep coming. She would have been pleased, I think, with her image that adorns the soon-to-be ubiquitous Golden Dollar Coin, debuting in March of 2000. Even before 1999 ended, the expensive, 24-karat gold commemorative Sacajawea Dollar Coin set sales records in America and abroad. The certificate with that commemorative coin correctly lists her death as having occurred on April ninth, 1884. I believe she would have also been pleased with that factual statement, which had no mention of the controversy pertaining to her friend Otter Woman's death in 1812.

I have dedicated this chapter to mentioning a small portion of the honors Sacajawea has received, to counteract the anti-Sacajawea venom that angers me. Feminists and revisionists that malign Sacajawea must remember that they are stepping on a lot of hearts that continue to revere her. I, for one, am not a hero-worshipper, except in one instance — Sacajawea. That has been so for forty-five years, or since, as a child, I saw her statue in the Public Square in my hometown, which happens to be Thomas Jefferson's Charlottesville, Virginia. As a sports broadcaster for many years, I traveled to many corners of America, never failing to be impressed by the numerous remembrances of Sacajawea that I encountered or sought out. Naturally, when I flew to Laramie in 1979 to broadcast the Wyoming—Richmond football game, I made a side-trip to visit Sacajawea's grave on the Wind River Reservation. I have never doubted where she is buried; my personal Sacajawea library, perhaps, is second to none.

To understand the depth of feelings many have for Sacajawea, I invite you to read the "Sacajawea" poem at the front of this book. It was written by Porter Bryan Coolidge in 1924. In his youth, Porter Coolidge lived on the Wind River Reservation within sight of Sacajawea's home. After she died in 1884, Mr. Coolidge very often laid her favorite flower, a rose, upon her grave. He did that one day in 1924 when he wrote the poem "Sacajawea" in honor of his "Indian girl with raven hair/O strangely sweet and darkly fair." In the first stanza he wrote: "And wildly sweet the melody/ Her tameless spirit sings to me."

Her "tameless spirit" sings to lot of us; that's why I will be damned before I will idly permit feminists and revisionists to defile Mr. Coolidge's "Indian girl with raven hair." And, as I have said, I believe revisionists who claim she died in South Dakota in 1812 are defiling her by robbing her of seventy-two years she graced this earth.

By the way, the poem "Sacajawea" by Porter Bryan Coolidge was published worldwide in many forms. In 1925 it was included in a London Times Feature Article entitled "Wyoming's Sacajawea Still Grips America." An Englishman named Frederick Bouthroyd read the poem in the London Times. He wrote a beautiful musical score to support Coolidge's lyrics. Bouthroyd then came to America, met with Coolidge and the song "Sacajawea" was born. On both sides of the Atlantic, it became a radio and stage hit, especially after it was recorded by the famed Eddie Cantor. So, you see, the feminists and revisionists who disparage Sacajawea should either tread lightly or expect some sharp rebukes. There are millions of us who will always be in love with Porter Bryan Coolidge's "Indian girl with raven hair/O strangely sweet and darkly fair."

Sacajawea's image, you see, is both irrepressible and irresistible to many of us. She fused the sacred and the secular but tilted toward basic, conscientious simplicity. Her intoxicating persona, I feel, still exacerbates the jealousy that hovers around the incomparable multitude of memorials that are still being heaped upon her. And her heavenly voice and terrestrial passion will always have resonance within millions of hearts, including mine.

"O strangely sweet and darkly fair, an Indian girl with raven hair" spawns mellifluous remembrances that will forever tower above the combined venom of all her detractors, including Blanche Schroer.

CHAPTER THIRTEEN

The oft-mentioned anecdotal "evidence" — namely, the three little Luttig, Brackenridge and Clark notes — is simply not enough to starkly reconstruct history. Groveling for complexities designed to reduce Sacajawea from a celebrity to a curiosity has created quandaries but no concrete answers, after all these years. But the core ingredient retains its historical edge — with the Shoshoni and U. S. Government positions regarding Sacajawea's longevity amply buttressed by diligent and key researchers from Dr. Grace Hebard to Dr. Charles Eastman.

Yet, her legend appears to be perpetually on the brink of being sabotaged by a feminist here or a revisionist there. She, like all historical figures, is not unassailable but the tenacity and resiliency of her character is truly remarkable, as the image of her genial, reassuring face on the upcoming Golden Dollar Coin will attest.

When it comes to Sacajawea, revisionists such as T. A. Larson, Blanche Schroer, Ken Burns and Steven Ambrose have simply been out-researched by lesser known historians, such as a true Sacajawea expert named Norman Dickinson of Riverton, Wyoming.

Back in the 1970s, Dickinson earned a solid reputation for debating Blanche Schroer face-to-face regarding when and where Sacajawea died. He, in fact, is credited with coining the phrase "The Enigmatic Sacajawea" even as he took giant steps to undermine the misinformation being dispensed by Schroer. Dickinson was a fine writer and speech-maker when it came to his passion — Sacajawea. On April fifteenth, 1975, he summarized his meticulous research in a long essay entitled "The Enigmatic Sacajawea," which first appeared in the Riverton (Wyoming) Ranger newspaper and later was widely reprinted as an historical document.[9 2]

He began that essay with this sentence: "It is interesting to note that Dr. T. A. Larson and Dr. Grace Raymond Hebard take varying viewpoints concerning Sacajawea."

Dickinson then detailed Sacajawea's life as well as anyone ever has. "A beautiful little Shoshone Indian girl lived in the area known as the Three Forks of the Missouri River or Beaverhead Valley region after her birth, probably in the year 1790," he wrote in his essay. "She was destined to be very lithesome and beautiful the rest of her life. In addition, she was smart. When she was about twelve the Minnetaree Indians raided her village. Her father and other kin were killed but she was made a captive and her brother, Cameahwait, escaped. In the next five years she was traded to first one tribe and then another until she became the property of the Hidatsa Indians of South Dakota. The Hidatsa gave her the name Sacajawea, which to them meant 'Bird Woman.' The name is Shoshone in origin and to the Shoshones it means 'Canoe Launcher' in its best interpretation. On October 26, 1804, the Lewis and Clark Expedition reached the Mandan Villages near Fort Mandan in North Dakota. They met a French-Sioux named Toussaint Charbonneau, a fur trapper. One of his squaws, purchased from the Hidatsas, was Sacajawea. Charbonneau, believed to have been born in 1768, was about thirty-two years older than Sacajawea, who was then in her early teens and pregnant. Charbonneau at the time had two other squaws, including a Shoshoni named Otter Woman, who was older than Sacajawea and was kind to her. A son named Jean Baptiste was born to Sacajawea on February eleventh, 1805. At that point, Lewis and Clark contracted with Charbonneau to be their guide. Charbonneau insisted on taking Sacajawea and the baby with them; Lewis and Clark, aware that a woman and a baby traveling with men signaled peaceful intentions to Plains Indians, agreed. But Lewis and Clark, over Charbonneau's objections, insisted he and Sacajawea had to be formally married. Clark performed the ceremony even as Charbonneau wailed that he had purchased his 'squaw' and she belonged 'only to him.'"

Much deeper into his noteworthy essay, Dickinson picked up

Sacajawea's life after she had emerged as the superstar of the now famed, two-year Lewis and Clark Expedition. Sacajawea and her two sons, Baptiste and the adopted Basil, were taken by Charbonneau, at William Clark's request, to St. Louis, where Clark was now the government's top Indian Agent on his climb up the political ladder.

"Clark," Dickinson wrote, "had a deep attachment for Baptiste and spoke of him as 'my son' or 'my boy' and this is why some writers maintain Clark was Baptiste's father. Clark also referred to Baptiste as 'Pomp' and so did Sacajawea. Pomp in Shoshoni means head or leader and refers to the first born. Charbonneau, with his squaws and sons Baptiste and Toussaint, Jr., arrived in St. Louis in August of 1806. Clark arranged for their quarters and put the boys in school. He also sold a small acreage and a cabin to Charbonneau. In April of 1811, after selling his property back to Clark, Charbonneau contracted with a fur company so he could return to the wilderness. He left on a boat up the Missouri with Otter Woman, leaving Sacajawea and the boys in Clark's care. The boys were simply too young to be separated from their mother, and Sacajawea was in love with Clark. Sacajawea soon received word that Otter Woman had died at Fort Manuel in December of 1812. Several times, alone and with Charbonneau, Sacajawea made feints to return to her Indian world. Prince Paul of Wurttemberg, on a visit to the U. S., met and grew fond of Baptiste. He got permission to take Baptiste back to Germany with him and, in the next six years, Baptiste received an European education and temporarily acquired white man's ways. Sacajawea had bounced back to Clark in St. Louis in 1823 when Charbonneau showed back up with a new squaw named Eagle. Eagle became very jealous of Sacajawea and continually urged Charbonneau to mistreat her. He did beat her one day, although Sacajawea stood up to him and then left him for good. Her sons also never forgave Charbonneau for beating their mother. Sacajawea ventured to the southwest and joined the Comanches, kinfolk to the Shoshones. She spoke French fluently and was long remembered by the Comanches because she prevented them from being cheated in trading deals. She married the Comanche Jirk Meat and was his wife for twenty-five years, bearing him five children. Two of the children, Ticannof and Yogawasier, survived to adulthood. Jirk Meat was killed in battle, after which Sacajawea piled brush on her lodge to indicate she would never return. She left the Comanches, taking her daughter Yogawasier with her. Her son Ticannof was grown and had his own Comanche family. Sacajawea was around sixty now but still quite pretty and agile. She drifted from place to place, including, for sure, towns such as Fort Hall and Virginia City and as far north as the Montana—Canadian border. She rode the stages and was not charged passage because she was known to everyone and respected for her contributions to Lewis and Clark. She had many names, as was common to Shoshoni women. She was generally known as Porivo, which means "Chief." Eventually she migrated to Fort Bridger in western Wyoming. We know this because at Fort Bridger she lived in a lodge near the government quarters and became a top aide to the Indian Agent. She also made robes and other articles and sold them to travelers. It was at Fort Bridger that Sacajawea reunited with her Shoshoni people again. She learned that her brother, Chief Cameahwait, had been killed in battle and Chief Washakie now was leader of the Shoshones. Basil, her adopted son, became extremely close to Sacajawea at Fort Bridger. Baptiste was in the area too, Basil said, but Baptiste was now a heavy drinker, which caused him to fall from Sacajawea's grace and, perhaps, drew her even closer to Basil. On July fourth, 1869, Sacajawea attended the famous Fort Bridger Treaty signing. She was asked to be a signatory but modestly declined and requested that Basil sign in her stead. He did. The Bridger Treaty created the Wind River Reservation, which became home to Sacajawea and Basil in 1871, with Baptiste an off and on resident, too. At Wind River, Sacajawea worked closely with key whites such as Agent F. G. Burnett, particularly because of her fondness for agriculture. She became very involved in beadwork but also crafted moccasins and robes, which she often sold to the public. During this period, Burnett described her as being fair in complexion, pleasant looking and weighing about 142 pounds. At Wind River, Sacajawea constantly wore the Jefferson Medal that the U. S. Government had given her. On April ninth, 1884, after little sickness, Sacajawea passed away during the night. The next morning, Indian Agent Lane said, 'Basil spoke to me with tears in his eyes, saying, 'My mother is dead.'"

Norman Dickinson's account of Sacajawea's life essentially parallels the Oral/Traditional History of the Shoshones as well as notable documentation in the white world from people such as government researcher Charles Eastman and the preacher, John Roberts, who officiated at her burial.

"Understand," John Tarnese told me, "that minor details of one's life during that period may provoke different renderings. But the major details of Sacajawea's life right up until 1884 line up clearly in the Shoshoni world, with sufficient corroboration from many white sources. In other words, either she lived beyond 1812 or she didn't. And if she did, she didn't die at Fort Manuel in 1812. The Shoshones knew the distinction between Sacajawea and Otter Woman, and it's clear some whites didn't. That's a shame, based on the problems it has created over the years."[9] [3]

CHAPTER FOURTEEN

My theme is simple but steadfast: The oral history of the Shoshoni people is more definitive and reliable concerning the duration of Sacajawea's life than the needlessly complicated scenario based on three little handwritten notes left behind in the white world.

However, there are innumerable corroborations of whites to substantiate the Shoshoni version. There are, for example, only two written documents that positively identify the elderly woman buried on April ninth, 1884, on the Wind River Reservation and both those documents were compiled by white authorities.[94]

One was dated November 1, 1877, and is the census roll of the Wind River Shoshone and Bannock Indians.

The other was dated April 9, 1884, and is the official death certificate of the elderly woman buried that day.

Both those documents very clearly refer to her as "Basil's mother." Basil, from the moment he was adopted by Sacajawea when he was a baby, had only one mother — Sacajawea.

There has never been any controversy concerning Basil's background or his high-profile and admirable position as a longtime Shoshoni leader on the Wind River Reservation. Also, no one disputes the fact that Basil's natural mother was Sacajawea's sister and that Sacajawea adopted him upon learning of her sister's death. It is very significant to emphasize that Basil had only one natural mother, Sacajawea's sister, and only one adoptive mother, Sacajawea herself.

While her natural son Baptiste, the famed "papoose," had adult problems with alcohol and drugs and his death is controversial, no such controversy surrounds the life and death of the highly principled Basil. His supreme devotion to Sacajawea is unquestioned in the Shoshoni world and staunchly supported by noted whites on the Wind River Reservation, such as Reverend Roberts, Superintendent Irvin and Agent Lane.[95] Could Basil himself have been totally fooled as to Sacajawea's true identity?

Beyond all that, there are many other whites that had connections to the Wind River Reservation during Sacajawea's lifetime and all knew for a fact that "Basil's mother" who died in 1884 was indeed the Lewis and Clark heroine. That list of whites includes: Elmo LeClair, John Enos, James McAdams, John McAdams, Sarah Irwin, Joseph Slade, Charlie Oldham, James Patten, William McCabe, Fincelious G. Burnett, Edward St. John, Charles Harrison and Bill Rogers.

From that stockpile of Wind River names who knew Sacajawea, let's examine "Fin Burnett." On May first, 1871, Fin became the Agricultural Minister on the Wind River Reservation and his job was to teach the Shoshones agriculture. Because Sacajawea was also deeply interested in agriculture, she and Basil were extremely close to Fin from 1871 until Sacajawea's death in 1884. As an intimate, Fin was gifted with Sacajawea's reminiscences of her days with the Lewis and Clark Expedition. "Many times" Fin was allowed "to hold" Sacajawea's beloved Jefferson Medal. And Fin was "abundantly familiar" with the letters and documents in Sacajawea's bag — letters and documents signed by Meriwether Lewis, William Clark and Brigham Young.

To his dying day, Fin Burnett never doubted that his "farming buddy" on the Wind River Reservation was the Sacajawea of Lewis and Clark fame. His granddaughters — Bernice Twitchell and Esther Horne — were great, great granddaughters of Sacajawea because their father was Fincelious Grey Burnett, Jr., and their mother was Millie Ethel Large, the granddaughter of Basil. Bernice and Esther meticulously studied Sacajawea's life and never for a moment questioned the day and place of her death — April ninth, 1884, on the Wind River Reservation. "Her best likeness," Bernice said many times, "is the statue by the sculptor Henry Altman. I love it so."

Esther said, "Our grandfather Fin was fond of telling us over and over again about what Sacajawea had told him regarding the trip up the Missouri River, the expedition's need of horses and their meeting with her people and her joy at seeing her brother, Chief Cameahwait. She spoke of the rough terrain on the western slopes and said because of the shortage of game the expedition members were once reduced to eating dog meat, but she said she would have starved before eating dogs, which had been purchased from Indians. She told of constructing canoes to travel down the Snake River and of trading the Indians for horses to get around shallow spots. Her brother, Chief Cameahwait, provided her a horse. When she would tell the story of the whale she saw she would laugh and then remind grandpa of the many times her Shoshoni and Comanche friends called that story 'ishump' ('a lie') when she described the whale as being as big as a house. We never tired of anything grandpa Fin had to say about Sacajawea and we have spent lifetimes determining and knowing that every word was the truth. He always told us to be proud of our Indian heritage because we were the great, great granddaughters of Sacajawea, the Indian girl guide of the Lewis and Clark Expedition. I am so heavenly proud of her, as all true Americans should be."[96]

Today on the Wind River Reservation there is a beautiful little Shoshoni girl named Tara Snyder — a direct descendant of Sacajawea. Tara loves to pick flowers and place them on Sacajawea's grave. If the Shoshones listened to noted but misguided historians such as Ken Burns, Steven Ambrose and T. A. Larson, Tara would have to go to South Dakota to pay homage to her cherished ancestor. But the Shoshones know exactly when Sacajawea died — in 1884 — and exactly where she is buried — on Wyoming's Wind River Reservation.[97] And that includes Tara Snyder, because her Shoshoni people would never mislead her about something as important to them as Sacajawea.

Time-Life Books has a recently published, twenty-two volume series of beautiful, hardback books entitled "The American Indians."

In the book entitled "Indians of the Western Range," the Time-

Life section devoted to Sacajawea includes, on Page eighty-six, a truly gorgeous, color picture of the little Shoshoni girl, Tara Snyder, with a bouquet of flowers at the huge marble shrine that honors Sacajawea near her gravesite on the Wind River Reservation.

The engraving on that magnificent shrine very correctly reads: "Sacajawea; died April 9, 1884; a guide with the Lewis and Clark Expedition, 1805—1806; identified by Rev. J. Roberts who officiated at her burial."

The updated and thoroughly researched Time-Life series correctly indicates when and where Sacajawea died and where she is buried. There is, also correctly, no mention of the South Dakota version of her death. Among the many true Indian experts who advised Time-Life on their splendid series entitled "The American Indians" is Frederick E. Hoxie. Hoxie is a trustee of the National Museum of the American Indian in Washington, D. C. and, among many other positions, was a key member of the Senate Select Committee on Indian Affairs. Hoxie's book — *A Final Promise: The Campaign to Assimilate the Indians 1880—1920* — is an absolute classic.

Lynn Pankonin — curator of the American Indian Collections for the Cheney Cowles Museum in Spokane, Washington — was also a key advisor on the accurate Time-Life Indian series. Pankonin has devoted her life to studying American Indians, specializing on the tribes in the western Plateau. She, like Hoxie, is a true Indian expert.[98]

My study of Sacajawea dates back forty years and includes, I believe, every major book or article or document depicting her life.

Over time, I have learned that the oral history of the Shoshoni people themselves much more accurately depicts Sacajawea's life than much of what is accepted as fact in the white world. Thus, I feel indebted to my Shoshoni friends such as John Tarnese.

However, to verify the oral history of the Shoshones I meticulously balance it out against any research, documentations or opinions in the white world. In doing so, I rely on true experts, such as Hoxie and Pankonin, and I am somewhat taken aback at how inaccurate the "anointed" historians — such as Ken Burns, Steven Ambrose and T. A. Larson — are in regards to Sacajawea.

Because Burns and Ambrose can literally saturate television to pimp any book or project they have coming out at any particular time, I believe they should be challenged, particularly in regards to an icon such as Sacajawea. She has, I believe, been in the crosshairs long enough. That's what this book is all about. If they are the anointed ones in scattering data about Sacajawea, I think Burns, Ambrose and Larson should at least be required to toe the line regarding historical facts and shape their opinions accordingly.

Even in the omnipotent age of television and computers, history should not be revised or distorted simply because "celebrity" historians go unchallenged as they exercise their privilege of freely pimping their works on television, radio, magazines, newspapers or Online.

And whether Sacajawea died in South Dakota in 1812 or in Wyoming in 1884 is a glaring disparity, to say the least.

CHAPTER FIFTEEN

Of the thirty-three members of the Lewis and Clark Expedition, it is not coincidental that the only two deaths that sparked controversy in the white world were those of Sacajawea and Pomp — the two Indians.

No one questions the fact that William Clark died on September first, 1838, at the home of his eldest son, Meriwether Lewis Clark. He had been named top Indian Agent for the West and also governor of the Missouri Territory. Also, he was a successful businessman. He had married Julia Hancock, whom he always called "Judith."[99]

Meriwether Lewis shot himself twice at Grinder's Stand, an inn south of Nashville, on October eleventh, 1809. Some historians believe Lewis was murdered but Thomas Jefferson and William Clark are among those who studied the circumstances and believed he committed suicide.[100]

York, William Clark's slave and the only Negro on the Lewis and Clark Expedition, died in 1831 of cholera. He had been Clark's dear friend, not just a slave, and he furiously saved Clark from drowning on the epic journey. Clark officially made York a free man a decade after the expedition ended and set him up in the freighting business in both Tennessee and Kentucky.[101]

York, by the way, was perhaps the first great Negro athlete. He was a tall, powerful and athletic man. On the expedition, Indians marveled over him, his physique as well as his black skin. In fact, the Indians were so enamoured of York that they insisted on inbreeding with him, gestures that York seldom spurned. He was offered Indian females, married and unmarried ones. As historian Steven Ambrose often points out, Indian husbands would stand guard outside while York conducted "his business" with their wives inside the teepee.[102]

The Lewis and Clark journals, buttressed by speeches that William Clark began to make in 1814 as he negotiated with publishers in Philadelphia, confirm these sexual invitations often kept York outside the campsites at night.[103] And, as noted earlier, the oral history of the Shoshoni confirms that Sacajawea herself "tried" York on at least one occasion.

It is also worth noting that both Sacajawea and York were allowed to vote on all matters requiring pertinent decisions on the journey. For example, the captains — Lewis and Clark — would employ and adhere to the democratic process when it came to such matters as where they would pitch camp or build a fort. So York got to vote six decades before slaves in the United States were emancipated and enfranchised. And Sacajawea got to vote more than a century before either women or Indians were granted the full rights of citizenship.[104]

John Colter, who gained fame as an explorer during and after the Lewis and Clark Expedition, died on his farm in Missouri in 1813. All male members of the Expedition were awarded 320 acres by the U. S. government, while Lewis and Clark got 1600 acres. Also, Lewis and Clark paid Charbonneau the sum of $533.33. Sacajawea informed Clark that she didn't want any money or land but just the "honor" of being a part of the journey. Clark accepted that but also made sure that the nation would never forget her contributions.[105]

Of the thirty-three members of the expedition, only one died during the journey. Sergeant Charles Floyd succumbed to a burst appendix on August twentieth, 1804, near what is now Sioux City, Iowa. That made him the first U. S. soldier to die west of the Mississippi.[106]

Other members of the expedition included such young men as John Ordway, a soldier from New Hampshire; Patrick Gass, an Irish carpenter from Pennsylvania; and Joseph Whitehouse, a tailor from Virginia. These three, and others like them, lived out their lives in normal and honored fashions. They were considered national heroes in their communities because the expedition was treasured from the moment it was completed. As the captains — Lewis and Clark — made their way to Washington to inform President Jefferson, balls and galas were held in every town they passed through. Lewis noted that one senator in Washington told him that it was as if he and Clark had "just returned from the moon." Jefferson and Congress quickly named Lewis governor of the Louisiana Territory while Clark was made the top Indian Agent for the West and brigadier general of the territory's militia.[107]

So, what happened to Jean Baptiste, the tiniest member of the expedition but surely one of the most famous because of his ubiquitous inclusion as the "papoose" on his mother's back as depicted by the numerous Sacajawea statues, memorials and paintings?

Well, much of his life is among the most chronicled in American history, beginning with his birth on February eleventh, 1805, at the outset of the famed expedition.

History records that the teenage Sacajawea had trouble with the delivery, until Lewis and Clark themselves concocted a potion from smashed rattlesnake rattles to speed the birth. Then history registers the fact that Clark nicknamed the baby "Pomp," which meant "first born" in his mother's Shoshoni tongue. Smitten with Clark, who was also smitten with both her and her baby, Sacajawea also called him "Pomp." And Clark, verbally and in written words, often called Pomp "my son" or "my boy."[108]

At journey's end — which comprised, by Clark's astute reckoning, 4,162 miles back and forth from the mouth of the Missouri to the Pacific Ocean — Pomp was nineteen months old. He was a special baby, especially in the eyes of Clark and Sacajawea. By the time he could walk, he was also a dancer that readily "performed" to the amusement of all.

A rock formation in Montana, Pompei's Pillar, is named after Pomp. It is an isolated rock 200 feet high on the south bank of the Yellowstone River. William Clark climbed that rock on July 25, 1806, and carved his name on it, a carving that is still very visible.

It was Clark who then named the rock formation after Little Pomp, whom he adored. It had long been used by the Indians as a lookout and as a point from which to send smoke signals, and it is now a national monument.[109]

Pomp's life into adulthood is also well chronicled because Clark, with Sacajawea's approval, insisted on providing him with the best education possible in the white world. So, both in St. Louis, Clark's hometown, and in Europe, where he first ventured with an admiring German prince, Pomp indeed was superbly educated, so much so that, upon his return from Europe, he could speak five languages fluently, including English, French, German and Spanish. Funded in the 1920s by Germany's Prince Paul of Wurttemberg, Pomp visited Germany, France, England and Africa.

Back in America, the now urbane, white-oriented Jean Baptiste Charbonneau exuded few hints that he was the famed "papoose" of Lewis and Clark fame. Still, he rode his celebritism into documented associations with noted western figures such as Buffalo Bill Cody, Kit Carson, Jim Bridger and John Charles Fremont.[110]

For a time, he was a successful guide and explorer on the frontier. When Sir William Drummond Stewart made his last hunting expedition into the Green River and Wind River areas, Pomp was one of his scouts.

It is known that Pomp attempted several reunions with his mother, Sacajawea, and his brother, Basil, in western Wyoming.[111]

But not only was he essentially white and they were thoroughly Shoshoni, the defining element in Pomp's adult life, they discovered, was whiskey, something that was anathema to Sacajawea. One of the great pains of her life was the belief that whiskey — "the white man's poison" — had reduced Pomp "to a ghost of a man." To her, Pomp was a white-educated drunk while the adopted Basil was, in her mind, the epitome of a decent, loving Shoshoni son.[112]

Pomp was in his mid-twenties when his six-year sojourn to Europe ended and not only was his natural mother Sacajawea but his legally adoptive father was William Clark, an extremely powerful man with dire influence over the burgeoning national interest in the western frontier. But, with all those advantages, Pomp seemed mired in a "no-man's land," caught between the culturally diverse tugs of the white world and the Indian world.

Slowly, Pomp's fame began to dissipate because the two pillars in his life — Sacajawea and William Clark — refused to accept him as a drunkard, and both were ashamed of him.[113]

By 1866, Pomp was more a half-breed frontiersman than a highly educated, urbane white man. Ravaged by whiskey, he indeed became ghost-like and his superb education, including his fluency in five languages, atrophied into nothingness as he drifted about on the fringes of white and Indian society, but neither was inclusive. Yet, his fame as the Lewis and Clark "papoose" never totally deserted him. Whites, culturally addicted to celebrities, fawned over him at times and often showered him with their presence and their gifts, including whiskey.

At periods in his adult life, especially when he was a productive member of some excursion or adventure on the frontier, Pomp was happy and healthy, and periodically safe from whiskey. But the "demon in the bottle," as the Shoshones recall, always managed to snare him anew.

In and around Fort Bridger, in western Wyoming, in the mid-1800s, Pomp several times reunited with Sacajawea and Basil. But his mother would not embrace "a whiskey-ravaged Pomp" and he, in turn, was quite jealous of the hold the impressive, whiskey-free Basil had on Sacajawea, Pomp's natural mother and Basil's adoptive mother.[114]

Estranged from Sacajawea, Pomp drifted further and further into vacuums by the 1860s. But stopovers with various Shoshoni bands indicated that he was trying to reshape his life into an image that his mother would, once again, cherish. In the meantime, Sacajawea and Basil were methodically and purposefully headed toward the primary Shoshoni encampment on the Wind River in central Wyoming.[115]

A century later, in September of 1970, an article penned by

Irving Anderson in the *Oregon Historical Quarterly* convinced most white historians that Pomp died on May sixteenth, 1866, on a ranch near Danner, Oregon. Like with the death of Otter Woman at Fort Manuel way back in 1812, somebody undoubtedly died on that ranch near Danner, Oregon, on May sixteenth, 1866. However, it was not Pomp. Countless times, for decades, there were false "sightings" of Pomp as well as Sacajawea in the white world, by whites who had never laid eyes on either one of them.[116]

On August 7, 1971, William Clark Andreon — the grandson of William Clark — spoke at the dedication of the Baptiste monument at Danner, Oregon. A huge, eight-foot, wooden marker still bears this inscription:

Oregon History

Jean Baptiste Charbonneau
1805—1866

This site marks the final resting place of the youngest member of the Lewis and Clark Expedition. Born to Sacajawea and Toussaint Charbonneau at Fort Mandan (North Dakota) on February 11, 1805. Baptiste and his mother symbolized the peaceful nature of the "Corps of Discovery". Educated by Captain William Clark at St. Louis. Baptiste, at age 18, traveled to Europe where he spent six years, becoming fluent in English, German, French and Spanish.

Returning to America in 1829, he ranged the far west for nearly four decades, as mountain man, guide, interpreter, magistrate and Forty Niner.

In 1866, he left the California gold fields for a new strike in Montana, contracted pneumonia enroute, reached "Inskip's Ranche" here, and died on May 16, 1866.

Regardless of how definitive that plaque in Danner, Oregon, appears, it remains highly controversial and is, in fact, erroneous.[117]

Historian Irving Anderson's meticulous research into the life of Jean Baptiste Charbonneau first culminated in that article entitled "J. B. Charbonneau, Son of Sacajawea," which initially appeared in the *Oregon Historical Quarterly* in September of 1970. It was Anderson and Anderson alone who pinpointed the famed papoose's death as having occurred in 1866 in Oregon.

Most white historians have accepted Anderson's conclusion as to when and where Pomp died, and where he is buried.

However, as with Sacajawea's death, the oral history of the Shoshones differs markedly with the white historians. As Indian expert Dr. Charles Eastman discovered in 1925 when the U. S. government assigned him to research Sacajawea's life, the oral history of the Indians was much more definitive than either notes or sightings reported in the white world. For example, Dr. Eastman noted that three different Indian tribes provided him with the exact same data on Sacajawea although none of the three tribes knew he was consulting the others.[118] With the Shoshones and their Indian cousins, such as the Comanches, word of mouth and campfire stories about Sacajawea and Pomp proved much more reliable than jottings or false sightings in the white world.

Shoshoni traditional history continues to maintain that Pomp reunited with Sacajawea on the Wind River Reservation and lived out his life there, dying in 1885 shortly after his mother passed away.

Official census records of the Wind River Reservation list a "Bat-tez" who was indisputably close to Sacajawea and was always called "Baptiste" by the Shoshones. But the census records do not register the name "Baptiste," convincing many that Pomp did die in Oregon in 1866 and was never with the Shoshones on Wyoming's Wind River Reservation.[119]

However, the Shoshones at Wind River knew "Bat-tez" and "Baptiste" to be one and the same. This is confirmed by many whites, including the Reverend John Roberts, who knew Baptiste, or Bat-tez, well. At one point in his life, Reverend Roberts mentioned the fact that "Bat-tez" did not "appear to be well educated" and that comment fueled controversy in the white world because it was well known that Baptiste was extremely well educated. However, Reverend Roberts tried mightily to explain his comment by stating that atrophy had eroded Baptiste's education because he had "never really used it for many years prior to his death in 1885."[1][20]

Some white historians still maintain that the Wind River Battez was not Baptiste and thus there was never a Wind River Sacajawea, just an old lady named Porivo, which was one of Sacajawea's several nicknames. That nickname, first bestowed on Sacajawea by the Comanches, meant "Chief Woman." But it's some whites, not the Shoshones, that are confused about the monikers "Bat-tez" and "Porivo." And that confusion, in the white world, has distorted the multitude of other Wind River-Sacajawea evidence that is beyond both dispute and confusion.

Beyond all that, it is Sacajawea's ties to her adopted son Basil, not to her natural son Baptiste, that indelibly places her on the Wind River on April ninth, 1884, the morning of her death.

Regardless of which side the white historians take on the Baptiste controversy, there is absolutely no controversy pertaining to Basil and that includes his decades-long attachment to his mother, Sacajawea, or to when and where he died and where he is buried.

Today, in the Indian Burial Grounds on the Wind River Reservation, Sacajawea's grave is in the middle of the sloping hillside, designated by the tallest headstone. The next two largest headstones, on each side of Sacajawea's, are Basil's and Baptiste's.

Basil is buried beside Sacajawea, just to her left. His headstone begins: "Basil, son of Sacajawea . . ." He died in 1886 and was first buried a few miles away at a spot where he had once had a vision about "crossing over." But soon, under the auspices of Reverend Roberts, the actual remains of Basil were disinterred and then reburied beside his mother, in keeping with the Shoshoni plan.

Just to the right side of Sacajawea's burial plot is the headstone that begins: "Dedicated in the memory of Baptiste Charbonneau, papoose of the Lewis and Clark Expedition, 1805—1806; son of Sacajawea . . . " Those words, the Shoshones believe, comfort Sacajawea in her eternal sleep although, while she aligned herself everlastingly to Basil, she didn't consider the Baptiste that returned from Europe in 1829 to be "the son I bore, the son I nurtured."[1 21]

Sacajawea felt the adult Baptiste had forsaken his Shoshoni roots and she was appalled that he had turned into a drunkard upon his return to the frontier.

However, to her dying day in 1884 Sacajawea lovingly cradled the memory of the papoose that she gave birth to on February eleventh, 1805 . . . the papoose that she carried for thousands of miles upon her back, right into the annals of American and Shoshoni history. Even after she could no longer accept the adult drunkard as her son, she never let go of the papoose, or of the young boy that William Clark legally adopted in 1813, when he also legally adopted Lizette, the infant daughter left behind by the death of Otter Woman.

In her precious bag—the one that contained the letters, documents and other mementos of her Lewis and Clark days—Sacajawea safeguarded another item, according to Shoshoni oral history and confirmed by various whites, including Sarah Irwin, within her inner circle. It was a "skull cap fashioned from rawhide and cloth." On the expedition, the infant Pomp had a habit of poking his head out from the blankets as he rode in the cradleboard attached to Sacajawea's back. One day he got a painful sunburn on his forehead. That night, Sacajawea and William Clark "cut and sewed" the skull cap to protect Pomp from the sun. Till her dying day, Sacajawea cradled that skull cap in her bag and, according to the Shoshones and Sarah Irwin, never a day passed that "she didn't pay homage to it."[1 22]

Most of the contents of Sacajawea's bag, as well as the beloved Jefferson Medal that she wore around her neck, are buried with her.

The skull cap, just a few days before she died, was removed and given to Maggie, Basil's daughter. According to Maggie and according to the oral history of the Shoshones, Sacajawea asked Maggie to make sure the skull cap was encased in an airtight rawhide covering and then placed near her heart when she was buried. Maggie, as later confirmed by Reverend John Roberts, kept that promise.

By the way, the "skull cap" that is a part of Shoshoni oral history was indeed crafted to keep the rays of the sun from scorching the infant Pomp's face and forehead when he traveled in the cradleboard on his mother's back. But many statues, as well as the new and celebrated dollar coin, depict the papoose facing in the same direction as his mother, stomach to back. However, Shoshoni mothers, including Sacajawea, designed the cradleboards so their infants would be back-to-back to them, not stomach to back. Thus, on the Lewis and Clark Expedition, as Sacajawea forged ahead, Pomp would have been looking behind her when he was not asleep, not in front of her.[1 23]

But I'm not here to quibble about which direction Pomp was facing when he rode in the cradleboard attached to Sacajawea's back.

In the next chapter I will, however, quibble with the white historians who maintain that Sacajawea died in 1812 in South Dakota and Pomp died in 1866 in Oregon while the Shoshones know they both died in the mid-1880s on the Wind River Reservation.

CHAPTER SIXTEEN

In 1838 and 1839, the Cherokee Indians in Tennessee, Alabama, North Carolina and Georgia were forced off their lands and moved to the barren Oklahoma Territory. That terrible blight on American history began in 1836 when General John E. Wool was sent from Washington, D. C., to that area to "ascertain the condition and probable designs of the Cherokee Indians." He knew that he was to lay the groundwork for the removal or annihilation of the Cherokees so whites could take over their land.

General Wool was told to expect to find uncivilized and mutinous savages. Instead, he found a Cherokee nation that firmly abided by a constitutional government. It had its own printing presses and very sophisticated newspapers; it owned but greatly respected Negro slaves; it had toll roads, ferries, gold mines and lavish plantations.

General Wool, a respected soldier for twenty-four years, reported his findings back to the U. S. Government and said he would be "filled with revulsion" if such a people "better and richer than we are" were destroyed "so us white people can steal their land." He was so firm that he asked to be relieved of his command.

The angered U. S. leader, President Andrew Jackson, immediately court-martialed General Wool. President Jackson then sent General Winfield Scott to lead a powerful army into the area for the purpose of rounding up the Cherokees and shipping them to the pre-selected, dusty, unwanted land out west. General Scott carried out his assignment and 15,000 Cherokees spent the summer of 1838 in harsh concentration camps, with 2,000 of them dying because of the horrible conditions.

In the fall of 1838, thirteen wagon trains arrived at Rattlesnake Springs, Tennessee, to begin the shipment of the Cherokees westward.

It began what is known to history as "The Trail of Tears" and, for a fact, the Cherokees wept bitterly from the outset of the forced march.

One of the harshest winters on record, the winter of 1838, hit the Cherokees unmercifully and another 2,000 of them died on the bitter trail. Many more of them would soon die of heartbreak or starvation once they were forcefully incarcerated in the God-forsaken no-man's-land that was so far removed from the plush homeland that had been stolen from them.[124]

I mention "The Trail of Tears" that is historically synonymous with the once affluent eastern Cherokees to illustrate a point regarding the Plains Indians in the West, Sacajawea's homeland.

When white settlers eventually coveted western land in the second half of the nineteenth century, much of that land was also occupied by Indian tribes that happened to be richer and more advanced socially and culturally than the whites. For example, the Nez Perce in the truly gorgeous and plush Wallowa Valley were more affluent, more decent and more honorable than any white settlement in the West in the 1860s and the 1870s. It was known, for instance, that the Nez Perce had never harmed a single white person and, in fact, had never failed to be extremely helpful to any whites they encountered. That even included the Lewis and Clark Expedition that fortuitously crossed Nez Perce territory and was not only befriended by the peaceful, wealthy Nez Perce but literally saved by them when hostile Indians, at one point, were very eager to wipe out the white intruders.[125]

In fact, a Nez Perce woman by the name of Watkuweis took it upon herself to keep a warring Indian party from attacking the Lewis and Clark Expedition, which was helpless at the time. Crossing the Bitterroot Mountains from Montana into Idaho in 1805, the expedition was surrounded by a large group of testy warriors when Watkuweis, with arms upraised, held them back. She told the would-be attackers that white traders had befriended her when she was a slave of the

Blackfeet and, she pointedly added, this group of whites included an Indian woman and an Indian baby to starkly indicate their peaceful purposes. Also, Watkuweis argued, it would be better to trade with these "peaceful whites" than kill them. Her argument ruled the day and the Lewis and Clark Expedition was spared. [126]

For sure — for themselves and for history — Lewis and Clark got the name of that Nez Perce woman — Watkuweis — and recorded in their journals her heroic, expedition-saving deed. Nuances sometimes determine who will be anointed historical celebrities and, certainly, the Shoshoni Sacajawea has been anointed. So should Watkuweis, the Nez Perce woman who saved the Lewis and Clark Expedition and kept Thomas Jefferson's vision alive.

Steven Ambrose, in his 1996 book, *"Undaunted Courage,"* wrote: "The United States owed more to the Nez Perce . . . than it ever acknowledged."

Yet, like with the Cherokees in the East, when white settlers coveted the lush Wallowa Valley, the home of the Nez Perce, armies were sent to dispel them. Driven from their lush land, where they alone had perfected the breeding of the magnificent and very unique Appaloosa horses, the Nez Perce — led by Chief Joseph — tried mightily to join Hunkpapa Sioux leader Sitting Bull, who was in exile in Canada.

In 1878, after ten heroic battles that somehow held the soldiers at bay, Chief Joseph was forced to surrender to General Nelson Miles within sight of the Canadian border. As he turned over his rifle, Chief Joseph left General Miles and American history with an unforgettable speech that ended with these words: "From where the sun now stands, I will fight no more forever."[127]

He kept his word. But the soldiers continued their marauding, stealing the Nez Perce land and shipping them off to waste away and die on dusty, barren reservations.

General Otis Howard, one of the soldier-leaders, along with General Nelson Miles and Colonel John Gibbon, that had unmercifully pursued the Nez Perce, quickly had a siege of conscience, reminiscent of General Wool in regards to the eastern Cherokees.

Howard, a one-armed veteran of the Civil War, fully realized that the affluent, peaceful and white-loving Nez Perce — led by the enormously intelligent and principled Chief Joseph — did not deserve to be destroyed. General Howard, with friends back in Washington, made arrangements for the eloquent Chief Joseph to present his case directly before the U. S. Congress. He did so with stirring words:

> *"They all say they are my friends and that I shall have justice but while their mouths all talk right I do not understand why nothing is done for my people. General Miles promised that we might return to our own country.*
>
> *I believed General Miles or I never would have surrendered.*
>
> *I have heard talk and talk, but nothing is done. Good words do not last long unless they amount to something. Words do not pay for my dead children. They do not pay for my country, now overrun by white men. Good words will not give my people good health and stop them from dying. Good words will not get my people a home where they can live in peace and care for themselves. I am tired of talk that comes to nothing. It makes my heart sick when I remember all the very good words and broken promises. You might as well expect the rivers to run backward as that any man who was born a free man should be contented when penned up and denied liberty to go where he pleases. Let me be a free man, free to travel, free to stop, free to work, free to trade where I choose, free to choose my own teachers, free to follow the religion of my fathers, free to think and talk and act for myself — and I will obey every law, or submit to the penalty."[28]*

The eloquence and righteousness of Chief Joseph brought many Congressmen to tears, but they were in the minority. He and his people were confined to barren reservations and by 1885 only 287 Nez Perce remained alive. Chief Joseph himself spent his final days on the desolate Colville Reservation in the state of Washington, mostly sitting beside campfires and dreaming of Wallowa Valley. He died, sitting by a campfire, on September twenty-first, 1904. The white doctor that voluntarily tended to him wrote in his official report that Chief Joseph had simply died "of a broken heart."[1][29]

The treatment of the Cherokees and the Nez Perce, I believe, can be equated with the arrogance and pomposity that white historians — especially the anointed ones such as Ken Burns, Steven Ambrose and T. A. Larson — have accorded the Shoshones. Who would, for example, question a white family when it merely registered the death of its cherished mother, particularly when there was no motive or incentive to lie or to deceive? During and after her death, all the controversies surrounding Sacajawea have festered in the white world, not the Shoshoni world. For too long, some high-profile white historians have told the Shoshones that their sheer superiority qualifies them to decide where and when Sacajawea and Baptiste died, and where they are buried. It seems to matter little that the Shoshoni position is starkly corroborated by the memories and records of numerous whites, pertinent whites with sharp insight and no reasons to mislead.

Like the Cherokees and the Nez Perce, the Shoshones are vastly out-numbered but not necessarily out-classed. The three Indian nations that knew Sacajawea best — the Shoshones, the Comanches and the Gros Ventres — all register the fact that Sacajawea lived a very meaningful life long after 1812, the date that many misguided but quite influential white historians say she died in South Dakota.[1][30]

John Roberts, the highly respected white preacher that knew her and buried her registers her death as April ninth, 1884, on the Wind River Reservation in Wyoming.[1][31]

Dr. Charles Eastman, the highly respected investigator for the U. S. Government, filed this report, which starkly corroborates Reverend Roberts and the Shoshones:

"She (Sacajawea) died April 9, 1884, and was buried by Missionary Roberts at Fort Washakie, Wyoming.

Not only the identity of Sacajawea, the Bird Woman, is proven by the accompanying testimonies taken in very wide parts of the country but they were taken in such a manner that they could not have known what other tribes knew and still they corroborated the truth of the history of her travels. Porivo or Chief Woman and Sacajawea, the Bird Woman, are one and the same person. She died on April 9, 1884, at Fort Washakie, Wyoming, and that is her final resting place."[1][32]

Having studied Sacajawea all my adult life, I agree with Dr. Charles Eastman, Reverend John Roberts and the Shoshones.

"We Shoshones," John Tarnese laments, "should own one of the television networks, I guess. I watched the Ken Burns documentary on PBS, where it was shown over and over again and said that Sacajawea died in 1812 in South Dakota. Because Ken Burns is a celebrity, all the other networks promote his work and thus, in the case of Sacajawea, promote his lie. But we Shoshones don't own any T-V networks, or big newspapers or publishing companies. So that one big mistake about Sacajawea proliferates, even if it is just casually dropped by a celebrity-type historian. It disappoints me, of course, but I understand. The very first Hollywood feature film was called "Squaw Man" and it was made in 1913. From then until the 1960s Hollywood turned out many, many more Cowboy and Indian films for movies and then television. Sadly, that provided a more indelible image of the Plains Indians than all the history books combined. I remind you that the movies didn't get it right very often and neither have some noted historians, especially when it comes to Sacajawea."

As John Tarnese indicates, even the most famous white historians, including Theodore Roosevelt, only got it (the history of the West) partially right. Roosevelt, the popular President and outdoorsman, wrote in his book *The Winning of the West* that "a number of instances are indelible blots on our fair fame; and yet, in describing our dealings with the Indians as a whole, historians do us much less than justice."

Yet, even Theodore Roosevelt wrote in his best-seller, "The tribes were warlike and blood-thirsty, jealous of each other and of the whites, and the young warriors were always on the alert to commit outrages when they could do it with impunity. With the best intentions, it was wholly impossible to evolve order out of such chaos without resort to the ultimate arbitrator — the sword."

Well, all the tribes were not "warlike and blood-thirsty" and this would certainly apply to the mostly meek and mild, and white-loving, Shoshones, Nez Perce and Cherokees. Still, "the sword" was applied to these peaceful, advanced civilizations as readily as it was used to subdue the more warlike bands.

When, for example, Roosevelt speaks of "jealous" Indians he could also turn that around and ascribe it to the whites. By the mid-1820s, for example, many whites in the East were quite jealous of the Cherokee Nation, a jealousy that set in motion acts of genocide that established a pattern that was replicated in the treatment of the Plains Indians. Why were many eastern whites jealous of the Cherokees? Well, by the mid-1820s the Cherokee Nation, with a population of 15,000, owned 22,000 cattle, 2,000 spinning wheels, ten saw mills, eight cotton gins, thirty-one grist mills and 700 looms, as well as 1300 black slaves. And they had a viable school system. Furthermore, the Cherokees had a mental genius named Sequoyah, for whom California's giant redwoods would later be named. Sequoyah is the only man in history to single-handedly invent a language for his people; that tribal language of eighty-two characters was used in the publication of the Cherokees' own newspaper, *"The Cherokee Phoenix."*

By 1827 the Cherokees were governed democratically by tribal delegates who drew up a very sophisticated constitution modeled on that of the United States. And the Cherokees democratically elected Chief John Ross to be their top leader. This was the affluent Cherokee Nation that was destroyed by the Trail of Tears, the forced march from their own land to the barren lands of Indian Territory.[133]

On the Great Plains, the Nez Perce and the Shoshones most closely resembled the Cherokees when it came to tribal affluence and peaceful intentions towards the whites.

"Our Trail of Tears," says Shoshoni elder John Tarnese, "continues to this day. And one subtle reminder of that is the controversy surrounding the death of Sacajawea. No matter what she did for the whites, she belongs to us. She came back to us and she died with us, on the Wind River Reservation in 1884. I feel, each time I read or hear where another white historian claims she died in 1812, that another little piece of her is being stolen from us, the poor but proud Shoshoni people."[134]

CHAPTER SEVENTEEN

For reasons that are sometimes hard to fathom, Sacajawea has garnered, over the decades, more than her fair share of detractors. This is so even though this Indian girl, born on the Great Plains in the eighteenth century, had a heart as pure as a mountain stream. Not once in her long life was she saddled with an ulterior motive to amass any measure of fame or fortune based on false pretenses or anything else. All she ever did, both as a girl and a woman, was to lead a dignified and productive life in total harmony with her own culture.[135]

When the fates dictated Sacajawea's immersion into the white world of the Lewis and Clark Expedition, she merely rode those waves with the grace and skill that defined her character, both before and after that historic journey reached out to her. She never asked for anything — certainly not glory or rewards — and she befriended a multitude of people, never hurting a single soul. As a mother, she was the epitome of a role model. In the last decades of her life, as an elder statesman on the Wind River Reservation, she was a dutiful and very eloquent instructor among her Shoshoni people in such productive areas as blanket weaving, agriculture and bead-making.[136]

Yet, posthumously, there are many people who have seen fit to disparage this most admirable of souls, although millions of us will forever cherish the ground upon which she so graciously toiled for so many years. In competition against every other American female that has ever lived, Sacajawea scored a convincing victory when the golden, heralded, 2000-year Dollar Coin was dedicated to her, with Eleanor Roosevelt coming in a distant second. That outcome was not surprising; the vitriol from Sacajawea bashers is.

Helen Clark, a meticulous student of the Sacajawea legend, wrote in 1967 in Near West Magazine: "She was, by all accounts, an admirable woman, possessed of virtues worthy of imitation — strong, physically and mentally; a good mother and wife; calm, self-possessed, courageous, long-suffering and resourceful; and gifted with that most cherished of favors, longevity."

Bonnie Hunter, in her famous book entitled "These Americans in Moccasins," is among the multitude of Sacajawea researchers that totally agree with Helen Clark. And Bonnie Hunter, in her notable book, diligently rebukes revisionists that dismiss the fact that Otter Woman, not Sacajawea, died at Fort Manuel in 1812.

"It is a known fact," wrote Bonnie Hunter, "that Charbonneau had several wives. Even the Lewis and Clark journals, and those kept by several of the other men of the expedition, refer to Charbonneau's 'women.' He brought three of his wives with him to the first big Christmas party the expedition held at Fort Mandan, the only Indians permitted to attend that particular celebration. We know that two of those women belonged to the Shoshone or Snake Indian nation; one was Sacajawea, the other was Otter Woman." [137]

Wyoming historian Blanche Schroer is a prime example of anti-Sacajawea, revisionists venom. In her famous and very influential essay — "Sacajawea: The Legend and the Truth" — Schroer wrote: "Sacajawea was not a guide as the subtitle of Dr. Hebard's book and a Daughters of the American Revolution memorial in her honor state. Her only real contribution in this area came on the single occasion, on the return trip, when she suggested the route over the Bozeman Trail. Even this information was not vital to the expedition's success. Art work and writings which depict Sacajawea leading the two geniuses of geography, Captains Lewis and Clark, westward across the land can only be termed laughable." [138]

In my opinion, it is Blanche Schroer, not Sacajawea, who is "laughable." That uncontested, venomous Schroer essay has startling prominence, to this day, in the Wyoming State Archives. I replicate it here (after using it in Chapter Twelve) to demonstrate my disgust over such anti-Sacajawea rhetoric from her adopted state, Wyoming.

While demeaning Sacajawea, superb historian Dr. Grace Hebard, the Daughters of the American Revolution and the Shoshoni people, Schroer heaps glowing praise upon Wyoming historian, T. A. Larson, for minimizing Sacajawea's standing as an American icon and discounting her connections to Wyoming's history. And the ramifications are stark. Thanks to Larson and Schroer, there is no national monument dedicated to Sacajawea in Wyoming; Sacajawea's grave is on a sloping, desolate hillside, which is difficult to locate.

Yet, unquestionably, Sacajawea is the most memorialized female in America's history. Months before the March, 2000, release of the golden Sacajawea Dollar Coin to the public, an expensive, 24-karat gold, commemorative, glass-encased edition attained astonishing sales, thanks to the fact that even foreigners — especially in Europe — remain starkly enchanted by America's greatest female legend. Correctly, the certificate accompanying that commemorative coin attests to the 1884 death of Sacajawea on Wyoming's Wind River Reservation. That is a fitting tribute to the Shoshoni people, and a fitting denunciation of the Sacajawea bashers who attempt to shorten her life by seventy-two years.

The place and timing of Sacajawea's birth and early childhood — in the Idaho-Montana region in the last decade of the 1700s — was, of course, beyond her control. But as an adult — after her Lewis and Clark days had earned her everlasting fame and captured the heart of the influential William Clark — Sacajawea had the option of where she might live, including Clark's hometown of St. Louis.[139] And she chose, for the last seven decades of her life, the area that became Wyoming Territory in 1876 and the State of Wyoming in 1890. Yet, Wyoming, to my mind, has displayed precious little pride in the Indian girl that is merely the most memorialized female in American history and the Indian girl that is cherished in many places around the world.

To further illustrate how ridiculous the anti-Sacajawea people are, presently one of the top-selling "Sacajawea books" is entitled: "Sacajawea and Company: The Twentieth Century Fictional American Indian Woman." It was written by Asebrit Sundquist and published in hardcover in January of 1991.

Nevertheless, the true legend of Sacajawea survives, just as she survived that awesome attack on her Shoshoni village when she was a child and just as she survived the rigors of the 4,000-mile Lewis and Clark Expedition when she was a teenager nursing her first baby. The legend of Sacajawea — the Sacajawea that William Clark and her Shoshoni people knew — will forever tower above all her detractors, because she deserves every statue, every memorial and every golden Dollar Coin that will ever be dedicated to her. The lifeline of her emotional buoyancy, I believe, is epitomized by the great 1924 poem by Porter Coolidge about his "Indian girl with raven hair/O strangely sweet and darkly fair . . ." The revisionists are not imperiling the Sacajawea legend; she's too profound for that. Rather, they belittle the sanctity, integrity and veracity of those who revere her, especially her own Shoshoni people.

As I have done earlier with the famous Luttig, Brackenridge and Clark notes, all serious data and research pointing to Sacajawea's alleged 1812 death at Fort Manuel in South Dakota must be closely examined. As you may have noted, I believe that all three of those little notes are explainable and, separately or collectively, they do not come close to providing incontrovertible proof that Sacajawea died at Fort Manuel in 1812. The 1811 Brackenridge note and the 1812 Luttig note don't even mention Sacajawea by name but they are the prime reasons some historians place Sacajawea on the boat heading to Fort Manuel in 1811 and dying at Fort Manuel in 1812. Brackenridge and Luttig merely and understandably confused Sacajawea with Otter Woman, another Shoshoni in her twenties who was the "Charbonneau wife" that died at Fort Manuel in 1812.[140] And William Clark, with his little 1826 note, could have been misinformed, could have been purposely covering Sacajawea's immersion back into Shoshoni society or he could have had various other reasons for scribbling that little notation. From 1826 till he died in 1838, Clark was never knowingly asked to explain his note and yet historical revisionists swear by it.

Buttressing the revisionists, I am aware that Dr. Ruth Hudson, a University of Wyoming professor, stated after Dr. Grace Hebard's death that Dr. Hebard told her that she would not have advanced her 1884 theory of Sacajawea's death had she known what she learned late in her own life. But Dr. Hebard, right up until her death in 1936, never officially recanted any of her Sacajawea research and she surely had ample opportunity to do so. As a dedicated historian, it is highly unlikely she would have made such a statement solely to Dr. Hudson.

Gwen Roberts, the youngest child of Reverend John Roberts, wrote that her father often said that the Wind River Bat-tez, whom the Shoshones claim was Sacajawea's son Baptiste, was "uneducated" while Baptiste was known to have been superbly educated.

Mildred Parker Yount, whose father was an officer on the Wind River Reservation when Sacajawea supposedly lived there, claimed her father said he never heard of Sacajawea during that period.

Playing Devil's Advocate, I asked John Tarnese, my expert on the Oral/Traditional History of the Wind River Shoshones, about the statements by Dr. Hudson, Gwen Roberts and Mildred Yount.

"Well . . . " John paused, closing his eyes a few moments before looking back at me. Then he continued. "Let me put it this way. The whites say it is tough to disprove a negative. But that's not really so concerning our history of Sacajawea. The Luttig, Brackenridge and Clark notes, I think, we have explained. Now comes the statements by the three ladies you mentioned — Hudson, Roberts and Yount. All right, I agree. You know your facts. The three notes and those three statements are probably the six things most used by those who say that Sacajawea died in 1812. But there are millions of things that her own people, the Shoshones, and the other two tribes she lived with, the Comanches and Gros Ventres, know to confirm she lived long after 1812. And that Indian version gets ample corroboration from many white sources — relating to intimate conversations with missionaries, officials at Wind River such as Lane, Irwin and his noted wife Sarah, Roberts and so forth. And Sacajawea's papers, signed by Lewis and Clark as well as Brigham Young, her other documents and, of course, her Jefferson Medal, simply can't be substantially disputed. And it's simple, she either lived beyond 1812 or she didn't. William Clark, the only white person out of those six who knew her and could distinguish her from any other Indian woman, jotted down two words in 1826 that indicate he was mistaken, being purposely deceptive or whatever. The other five can be dismissed as hearsay or simple misreadings from whites that didn't remotely know Sacajawea from any other Indian woman. We've said all along that only Shoshones and whites very intimate with Sacajawea would ever remotely share her Lewis and Clark connections. Then and now we Shoshones hear or read claims from time to time that she was an Hidatsa or something. Then and now the Shoshones never stressed her Lewis and Clark days. So we have never been motivated to lie about her and, from an ancestral standpoint, we surely are not inclined to be greatly mistaken about her. Basil, her beloved son, buried her, for God's sake. Two people, Basil and Basil's daughter Maggie, watched her die. Did they not know their beloved mother and grandmother? Or did some whites who never laid eyes on Sacajawea know her better than Basil, Maggie and all the others did? I will put it this way, about whether Sacajawea died in 1812 or in 1884. Rumors could crop up about anyone's death but if that supposed dead person was later seen and proved to be alive, the rumors should be finished off. Let's consider this. Twenty people were outdoors at a picnic last night when a truly prominent shooting star blazed across the heavens, horizon to horizon. Ten of those twenty people happened to be looking toward the sky and saw the shooting star, and said so. But the other ten were looking at the ground and never saw the shooting star, and said so. Now . . . let me ask you, did that shooting star blaze through the sky? Or, because ten of the twenty people weren't looking at the sky and thus didn't see it, does that mean there was no shooting star? That's what I mean by saying that Sacajawea either lived beyond 1812 or she didn't. We know she did, because the Shoshones knew her and could distinguish her surely from Otter Woman or anyone else. In other words, there are countless people who saw Sacajawea's star blaze across the Western sky from 1812 till 1884. Because Luttig, Brackenridge, Yount and those others weren't looking toward the sky, and also didn't remotely know Sacajawea from Otter Woman, do their words or notes signify that Sacajawea died in 1812? Do those little, explainable 'facts' outweigh all those people who knew Sacajawea and saw her shooting star until 1884? Are the Shoshones supported by the white preacher who buried her and by the federally funded investigation? If, Mr. Haney, I sound frustrated at times it's because I, and the Shoshones, feel some whites that didn't know Sacajawea and haven't researched her very well have far too much basically unchallenged leverage when it comes to one of our own. I will put it this way and then be done with it. Say, you spoke with your brother and then watched him enter a restaurant. Then your sister comes along and didn't speak to your brother and didn't see him enter the restaurant. Does that mean he didn't enter the restaurant?"

I could easily detect that John Tarnese was indeed frustrated. The tape recorder continued to run but there was a long pause, with John gazing down at his lap. Finally, he looked back at me.

"The controversy that hovers over Sacajawea's grave," he said, slowly, "is not her fault and not our fault. I am left to wonder, sometimes, if the furor disturbs the peaceful, eternal sleep that she so richly earned. But I am comforted, and I hope she is, by the love, respect and admiration that continues, after all these years, to come her way. She was special, very special. No one can ever take that away from her, or from us. As I grow old, I am amazed at the honors that still come her way. I am saddened by the controversy that still dogs the beautiful footprints she left behind on the western landscape and on the hearts and souls of her many admirers."[1][41]

CHAPTER EIGHTEEN

If one were to minutely study the history of the United States from 1607 — the date of the first permanent English settlement at Jamestown, Virginia — to the year 2000, one might conclude that three advanced Indian nations — the Cherokees, the Nez Perce and the Shoshones — were the three societies that were the friendliest and most helpful to the white Americans. France, back in colonial days, was an invaluable military ally as America broke free from England, of course, but France's motive was strictly self-serving.[1 42] That was not so with the more unselfish Cherokees, Nez Perce and Shoshones.

The Cherokees, Nez Perce and Shoshones have something else in common: When the whites coveted their land, they were annihilated or subdued on reservations so whites could take over their land.

I have touched on the indisputably tragic situations concerning the Cherokees and their Trail of Tears as well as the Nez Perce and their holy, eloquent leader, Chief Joseph. But all Indian nations, including the white-loving Shoshones, suffered the same fate when it came to occupying land coveted by whites.[1 43]

Vine Deloria, Jr. — in his book "Behind the Trail of Broken Treaties," which was published in 1974 by Delacorte Press — said, "The Cherokees, Creeks, Choctaws, Chickasaws and Seminoles — known as The Five Civilized Tribes — were all forced to sign treaties and move west. But in the treaties they insured that removal would never happen again. Since the 1830s the Five Civilized Tribes had become very strong, and had created small republics with schools, courts, businesses and even plantations."

As Deloria points out, all such treaties were broken when it suited the whites. Deloria is an Indian, a Standing Rock Sioux, who happens to have a passel of degrees from white universities — including a law degree from the University of Colorado. I, a white conservative, agree with his depiction of Indian treaties. In his aforementioned book, Deloria writes, "The responsibility of any nation, and the particular responsibility of elected officials of any nation, is not to justify what has passed for legality but to anticipate the conditions and problems of tomorrow and attempt to deal with them. The current confusion and violence in Indian country are a result of the failure to do so by generations of elected officials in this country. To continue to perpetuate myths about American Indians which have no basis in fact or in law is merely avoiding the larger issues confronting the nations of the world."

Although Deloria does not touch on the broken treaties involving the overly friendly Shoshones, he could have and his statement above still could apply to the government's treatment of the Shoshoni nation as well as the disrespect some noted white historians display regarding the Shoshoni Oral History pertaining to Sacajawea.

From time to time, white leaders — many of whom, of course, were or are highly principled people — have profusely apologized to various Indian tribes, especially the Cherokee and the Nez Perce.

In 1974 the U. S. Government gave the Cherokees $5 million, with some of the money going to descendants of the Cherokees who walked the Trail of Tears but a lot of the money merely going to white lawyers.

In 1987, as the 150th anniversary of the Trail of Tears was noted, North Carolina's governor, James Martin, gave a teary apology to the Cherokees in the town of Cherokee, North Carolina. As quoted by United Press International, Governor Martin said, "It is painful to say, but the Trail of Tears serves as a monument to man's inhumanity to man. It will live forever as a dark spot in American history."

Wilma Mankiller, the powerful chief of the Western Band of Cherokees in Oklahoma, was in Cherokee, N. C., that day. She took the podium and said, "I will always feel that Cherokee, North Carolina, is my home. We have a lot of history here. Whether we live in Oklahoma or North Carolina, whether we're rich or poor, we all have one thing in common — the Trail of Tears. The heirs of both the victims and the perpetrators of that event must always share it."[144]

Wilma Mankiller is correct but the many Trails of Tears apply to all the Indian nations, not just the Cherokees, in one form or the other, and that includes Sacajawea's Shoshones. When 15,000 affluent Cherokees had their plush lands stolen in North Carolina, Georgia and Tennessee, 4,000 of them died on the forced march to barren lands in Oklahoma, and most of the rest died there of malnutrition, disease, exposure and broken hearts. The Trail of Cherokee Tears passed through nine states — North Carolina, Georgia, Tennessee, Alabama, Kentucky, Illinois, Missouri, Arkansas and Oklahoma. All nine of those states apologized to Chief Wilma Mankiller on the 150th anniversary of the Trail of Tears. But sadly, none of those states, on behalf of the U. S. Government, could unring a bell.[145]

The Nez Perce, the affluent and white-loving owners of the lush Wallowa Valley, had their Trail of Tears in 1877 when whites coveted their land. That famous and circuitous trail ended just shy of the safe haven of the Canadian border when Chief Joseph finally surrendered to General Nelson Miles in order to save his few remaining women and children.

The Cherokee and Nez Perce Trails of Tears are embedded in our history, and this is not an attempt to rehash vicious indictments of whites regarding regrettable and uncontested facts.

But John Tarnese, my Shoshoni friend and a chronicler of the Oral History of the Shoshones, reminds me that, "We have our Trail of Tears, too, although white historians mostly emphasize that the Shoshones fought with western soldiers and then were rewarded by the government."

"It is often overlooked," John added, "that Shoshoni treaties with the government were routinely broken when it suited the whites. I invite you, for instance, to study the government records concerning The Treaty of Ruby Valley. I think, if you do, you'll find that it will shed light on how some white historians get away with falsehoods about the Sacajawea that you, and many others, admire so much."[146]

I accepted John's challenge and studied the government records concerning The Treaty of Ruby Valley.[147] It's an 1863 treaty the U. S. signed with the Western Shoshones.

In 1863, the government sought a rail route from the California gold fields to replenish the Civil War-drained U. S. Treasury. The white-friendly Shoshones signed the treaty to allow the railroad to be constructed through Shoshoni land. It was a typically kind gesture from the Shoshones; but no land was sold and no money or any other gratuity exchanged hands. In fact, the Shoshones did not believe that land could be bought or sold and the treaty clearly stipulated that the Shoshones would "forever" own their land.

Forever lasted until whites wanted the land. In blatant violation of The Treaty of Ruby Valley, whites claimed the land and both the U. S. Indian Claims Commission and the Supreme Court upheld those claims. The Shoshones, of course — like the Cherokees and the Nez Perce — weren't exactly represented on the Claims Commission or the Supreme Court.[148]

The Ruby Valley Treaty, to this day, has never been changed or repudiated, including that word "forever." But that 24 million acres of land was stolen from the Shoshones, as the U. S. Government admits.

Once, the government offered the Shoshones $26 million — the 1872 value of the land. The Shoshones refused that offer; lawyers, as typical in white capitalism, still took $2.5 million off the top of that offer, a very spendable $2.5 million although the Shoshones never got a cent.[149]

In 1973, two Shoshoni sisters — Mary and Carrie Dann — were still living on their ancestral land. The still existing Treaty of Ruby Valley guaranteed them "undisturbed use" of their traditional lands "forever." But in 1973 the Bureau of Land Management accused the Dann sisters of "trespassing on BLM lands." The sisters resisted, citing The Treaty of Ruby Valley and pointing out that not one line of the treaty had ever been changed or repudiated by either side.

The case went all the way to the U. S. Supreme Court; the Dann sisters, not surprisingly, lost. That "legal" proceeding does, to this day, include the statement from Shoshoni elder Glenn Holly: "Nothing happened in 1872. No land was taken by the government. We never lost that land, and we're not selling it. In our religion, it is forbidden to take money for land. What's really happening is that the U. S. Government is stealing the land from us right now."

Those two elderly Shoshoni sisters — Mary and Carrie Dann — still refused to vacate the land. Their stance, perhaps, can be equated to the position Rosa Parks took in 1955 in Montgomery when she changed history by refusing to give up her bus seat to a white man.

On November 19th, 1992, the U. S. military closed off media access to the Dann Ranch and then launched an assault on the property. As the livestock was being rounded up, a male member of the Dann family poured gasoline over himself and ignited it. He was subdued, beaten up and then charged with "assaulting federal officers." Carrie Dann herself — an elderly and tiny Shoshoni woman — rushed out to protest. She was . . . unmercifully beaten.[1 50]

If you conveniently have forgotten this 1992 event, or don't know about The Treaty of Ruby Valley, media accounts as well as accurate government records are readily available. Glenn Morris, in a widely circulated newspaper column in 1993, wrote this exact sentence: "The federal invasion (of the Dann Ranch) also assaulted Carrie Dann."

Glenn Morris concluded his syndicated newspaper article with these exact and telling words: "We are witnessing another shameful chapter of U. S. Indian policy being written — in your name.

Call the president. Call your senators. Call your representative. Tell them that these actions do not represent you or your family. Tell them to stop it. Tell them to leave the Shoshones alone and to honor The Treaty of Ruby Valley. This time there are no excuses. This time you cannot blame your ancestors. If you let it happen this time, the blood is on your hands."

No one, to my knowledge, has ever challenged the veracity of Glenn Morris' account of what happened on the Dann Ranch.

Because the assault on the Dann Ranch occurred in the 1990s, on our watch, Morris is correct when he states: "This time you cannot blame your ancestors. The blood is on your hands." The blood he speaks of belonged to Carrie Dann, an elderly Shoshoni woman. She was born and reared only in the U. S. and was as much a citizen as any of us. On June 2nd, 1924, the U. S. Congress got around to granting full citizenship to "all American Indians."[1 51]

As John Tarnese maintains, his Shoshones have had their own Trail of Tears.

"Some white historians," John adds, "are still treating Sacajawea the way the government soldiers treated Carrie Dann. It doesn't matter, it seems, whether the Shoshones are right or wrong. It only seems to matter who publishes the newspapers and the books and who makes the documentaries. At the moment, it appears that a few very high-profile historians have decided that our Sacajawea died in South Dakota in 1812 and is buried there. Does it then matter that she actually died in 1884 on the Wind River Reservation in Wyoming, and is buried there?"[1 52]

In the next and concluding chapter, I will recount the final moments of Sacajawea's life, including the last words she spoke and the last words she heard and the last significant gesture she made. This is the Shoshoni version of her death, the correct version.

I sincerely believe, the last moments in the life of the most memorialized female in American history are very important. For sure, they are important to the few thousand remaining Shoshones, Sacajawea's people. And they are important to millions of non-

Shoshones, those of us who will forever cherish her memory and try, as best we can, to defend the unique image she carved into America's soul.

CHAPTER NINETEEN

"Permit me to explain," Shoshoni elder John Tarnese told me near the end of an all-night, pre-arranged session in Laramie, "why, as Shoshones, we feel so strongly that, of all people, Sacajawea should not be shortchanged out of seventy-two years of her life. You say this tape has guided you to the final chapter of your book, the chapter wherein you reveal the Shoshoni version of her death — including her last spoken words and her final gesture, which pertained to the Jefferson Medal that for decades so closely tied her to the American people. Well, you see, Mr. Haney, she was an integral part of this country's greatest exploratory adventure, the Lewis and Clark Expedition that concluded in 1806. The West was a vast, uncharted wilderness then and it still was in 1812, when the revisionists such as Larson, Burns and Ambrose say she died. But by 1884, when she really died, the West was settled and very much charted, with the Lewis and Clark Expedition being the beacon for all that. You see, the Sacajawea that was born in the wilderness about 1790 would have died in the uncharted wilderness, if she had died in 1812. But by living to 1884 she lived to see that vast wilderness tamed, pointing the way to the true greatness of the world's greatest country. In other words, it justified the fruits of her labors and her contributions to it all. Heck, in 1879, when she was still very much alive, Thomas Edison had invented a workable electric light in his Menlo Park, New Jersey, office. Other Edison inventions, such as his 1877 phonograph, were changing the face of American civilization. At the Burns Store, which Sacajawea frequented for years on the Wind River Reservation, she actually heard a musical recording played for her. After that, in very fluent English and French, she said, 'My God! What's next?'

By then, she knew the telegraph had connected every community with all others, as had the railroads, which came to her Wyoming area in the late 1860s and then transcended the entire continent coast to coast. She even heard talk of telephones, horseless carriages and even flying machines. She loved newspapers and magazines, especially the photographs that newspapers and magazines had very prominently featured since the Civil War in the early 1860s. Yes, she lived long enough, till 1884, to see the West and America progress rapidly from the 1806 completion of the Lewis and Clark journey that featured her. But, had she died in 1812, she would have lived her entire life in the wilderness, because even the St. Louis that she had come to know soon after the journey was then just a frontier town on the edge of the wilderness. So, we Shoshones believe, if the revisionists take those seventy-two years from Sacajawea, from 1812 to 1884, it leaves her with a restless spirit. We are pragmatists. We realize the revisionists will continue to hound her spirit, so the prognosis isn't pretty and, perhaps, she will never be totally vindicated for the entire ninety-six years she spent on this earth. But, as you know, her spirit is not that of a shrinking violet and thus not likely to be cowed. The resiliency of her spirit, I believe, is revealed anew by her image on the celebrated Dollar Coin that will be out in March of the year 2000. The revisionists will always have problems diminishing Sacajawea's indomitable spirit. That's all I have to say and I appreciate your listening to, and verifying, the Shoshoni version of her life as well as her death, which was much more timely, from a longevity standpoint, than the revisionists say it was." [153]

Those are the last words I have on tape from John Tarnese. They remind me of Porter Coolidge's great poem, especially the last six lines that seem to underscore why, to so many, the spirit of Sacajawea is so indomitable and resilient:

"Now sunset's golden dreams are dead.
The Indian girl from me hath fled;
Still linger in the star-lit skies
The dusk and splendor of her eyes;

And voice of distant waterfall
Sweet echoes of her song recall."

I will admit that I intended this book as a loving portrait of a
paradoxical figure, but that does not mean it is biased. The only
paradox, or controversy, surrounding Sacajawea concerns whether
she died in 1812 in South Dakota or in 1884 in Wyoming. And it
is unfair to blame her for dying or not dying in 1812. Even if she
had died in 1812 it would in no way diminish the image I and
millions of others retain of Porter Coolidge's "Indian girl with raven
hair/So strangely sweet and darkly fair." Thus, there is no preju-
dice involved when I starkly agree with the Shoshones that she
died in 1884.

Despite attempts by revisionists to poke holes in the Sacajawea
mythology, she will never be a faint afterthought in the annals of
American history. At the dawn of a new millennium, the fabric of
our society seems to fray around us, with our maternal ethic perhaps crumbling a bit. But Sacajawea remains a living symbol of
America's lost values — discipline, loyalty, parenting, persistence
and so forth. I do not advocate worship, just a proper reverence of
the image that she crafted and people like Porter Coolidge molded.
Anything less will provoke the ire of those of us who respect what
she did for this country and revere everything she still stands for.

***

What now follows is the Shoshoni version of Sacajawea's death as
painstakingly told to me by Shoshoni elder John Tarnese. It is the
version that I deem to be correct, and the version corroborated by
many sources in the white world, as I've earlier tried to delineate.

You'll note that the Shoshones and I depict Sacajawea's death
as occurring in the early hours of April ninth, 1884, on the Wind
River Reservation while notable revisionists such as T. A. Larson,
Ken Burns and Steven Ambrose claim she died in 1812 in South
Dakota. Well, "notable" or not, the essence of their simple mistake

is that Larson, Burns and Ambrose confuse Sacajawea with Otter Woman, who was the other Shoshoni woman married to Charbonneau in 1812.

And so, here now is how the Shoshones register the last seven decades of Sacajawea's life, a life that I and many others believe has inspired more poems, more statues and more memorials than has any female in all of America's history. For that fact alone, I think, historical revisionists should take piercing reflections, or at least provide substantial proof, before challenging the proud Shoshones in regards to their most beloved ancestor.

***

By the 1830s, Sacajawea was with her Shoshoni people in the Green River area in what is now western Wyoming. The Shoshones were closely tied to their Comanche cousins and Sacajawea fell in love with a Conmanche warrior named Jirk Meat. She was his loving wife for twenty-six years and gave him five children, till he was killed in a battle with a rival tribe.

Three of Sacajawea's children with Jirk Meat died in infancy but two — a boy named Ticannof and a daughter named Yoga-wasier — survived into adulthood. Because Sacajawea's method of mourning the death of Jirk Meat differed from that of the Comanches, she returned to the Shoshones, agreeing to leave the grown Ticannof with his relatives but taking her daughter, Yoga-wasier, with her.

Meshing back into the Shoshoni world, she lived on the edge of the ever-encroaching white society, which didn't intimidate her.

A skilled and fervent bead-maker, she often sold her beads to whites. Her travels, at times, were with whites, even on stage-coaches. Several times, among whites and Shoshones, there is stark evidence that Sacajawea was given free passage on stagecoaches because of "the debt the whites owed her."[154]

The Shoshones say, and white history tends to agree, that Sacajawea traveled part of the way to Fort Bridger with the famed

John C. Fremont Expedition in July of 1843. At Fort Bridger, she was so well known to whites that she was given free supplies and offered free stagecoach rides to future destinations. During this period of her life, she hung around settlements such as Fort Bridger long enough to sell her beadwork and to get re-supplied with materials.

While she was at Fort Bridger, a famous treaty was signed between the Indians and whites. To honor her, one of the undisputed signatories of that famous treaty was her beloved, adopted son Basil.

During this time, a footnote was registered at Foot Bridger stipulating that Sacajawea was "5-foot-6, 132 pounds" and Basil was "a burly 6-foot, 200 pounds."[155]

From Fort Bridger in western Wyoming, Sacajawea and Basil slowly migrated with the Shoshones to central Wyoming, where they would live out their finals days on the Wind River Reservation.

Sacajawea did not fade gently into the night after the Lewis and Clark Expedition ended in 1806, or even after her final separation from William Clark, probably in the spring of 1821. Her intelligence and charisma wouldn't permit that, even back among the Plains Indians, who had no desire or inclination to dwell on her fame over in the white world. As noted earlier, Reverend John Roberts officially stated to the U. S. Government in 1835, "opprobrium" and "scorn" would have been heaped on Sacajawea within her own culture had she been heralded as being that closely identified with the whites.

The sagacious Sacajawea, however, was never a shrinking violet or a wallflower. On the Wind River Reservation, for example, she expressed her opinion about the government's treatment of Indians. Whites such as Sarah Irwin recalled that Sacajawea was surprisingly knowledgeable about such things as the Sand Creek Massacre down in Colorado in 1864 and Sitting Bull's return from exile in Canada in 1881. At the convent in St. Louis, Sacajawea had brushed up on English and she relished reading newspapers or having them read to her by favorite missionaries. She also devoured pictures, which were regular features in newspapers beginning with the Civil War in the early 1860s.

Sarah was also shocked that Sacajawea could converse about such things as Manifest Destiny, correctly applying to that multifaceted doctrine a definition that the white world still shied away from. To Sacajawea, according to Sarah and the Shoshones, Manifest Destiny meant that "the whites believed it was their God-given right to slaughter native inhabitants of any land they coveted to clear the area for themselves."[1 56]

Although Manifest Destiny was the brainchild of such great men as Thomas Jefferson, it seems that Sacajawea was among the first that was brave enough and astute enough to correctly label it.

On the Wind River Reservation, as she lived out her life with the blessed gift of longevity, Sacajawea's fertile mind and latent energy manifested itself in many ways. For example, the Shoshones to this day credit Sacajawea with markedly improving the agricultural situation on the Wind River Reservation. She was a firm believer in the age-old symbiosis of the crop system that the Indians called "the three sisters." In vegetable terms, the three sisters went by the names of squash, corn and beans. Sacajawea realized, and stressed to her people, that squash, corn and beans should be planted in related mounds. The broad leaves of the pumpkins inhibited weeds, the cornstalks would support the growing bean vines and, in turn, the beans and vines would send legumes of corn-nourishing nitrogen back into the soil. She had learned the word "nitrogen" from Mormons but defined it as "sugar to sweeten the soil and keep it happy."

Only in her nineties did Sacajawea grow feeble, and she did so under the watchful eyes of her adopted son, Basil. He respected her independent ways as long as he could but then tenderly moved her into his own house so that he and his family could lovingly tend to her needs.

Basil's home, as it awaited a monumental moment in history

— the death of Sacajawea — was listed as "Lodge 117" on the government's official ledger sheets. Many Shoshones and whites on the Wind River Reservation, generation to generation, have attested to this change in Sacajawea's life, when she reluctantly capitulated to being cared for by Basil's large family. Even then, there were many Shoshones and whites on the Wind River Reservation who simply never associated Sacajawea with the Lewis and Clark Expedition. Her connection with that historic event was never emphasized and memories of it were only shared with close intimates, both Shoshoni and Caucasian. She was rarely called Sacajawea, Porivo or any of her other Indian names. Her relatives called her "Mother" and almost everyone else on the Wind River Reservation referred to her as "Basil's Mother." Even on official documents she was usually depicted merely as "Basil's Mother."

Sacajawea suffered little in her old age. In the early morning of April ninth, 1884, she awakened and called out to Maggie, one of Basil's grown daughters and Sacajawea's favorite granddaughter. She asked for a cup of water. Maggie, for whatever reason, awakened Basil and suggested, "This time, father, I think your mother needs for you to take her this water."

Basil took Sacajawea the last thing she ever asked for — that cup of water. She raised her head and used "both hands to consume it."

With her head back on a straw pillow, and with a lamp beside her bed, she smiled up at Basil, who was now seated beside her. Sensing that the end was near, Maggie stepped discreetly back into the darkened doorway and just stood there observing, her presence unbeknownst to either Basil or Sacajawea. A week apart, Basil, who didn't even know Maggie had been standing back in the doorway, and Maggie would give exactly the same account to various relatives of Sacajawea's passing.

"I am fine," Sacajawea said, "but I am tired. Oh, son, I am . . . so much tired. Please believe that I deserve the long, peaceful sleep that awaits me. Make it so that others understand that . . . I am fine, just tired. Even this night I am not sad." A little smile descended on her lips. "My dreams have been good dreams. Before I called out for Maggie, I was young again. I was by a creek. Pomp was in his cradleboard against a log. Red was with me. We needed fish for supper. We caught three. I remember . . . we caught three . . . that day that seems . . . like . . . just . . . yesterday."

Her voice trailed off and her head turned slightly, as her tired eyes blinked softly up at the ceiling. The little smile still adorned her face and the remnants of that dream lingered with her. Basil and Maggie knew, to Sacajawea, "Red" meant the red-haired William Clark. As the seconds ticked away, she was blessed with a fond memory from her storied past.

Her eyes blinked slower and slower, and then closed gently. Basil, sitting at her left side, took her left hand in both of his. Her eyes opened and she smiled at him. "Be brave for me, son," she said. "I have tried so hard . . . for so long. Do not now be sad for me."

"I will try, mother," Basil said. "But of all who have walked this earth, you are the most special."

He leaned down, kissing her forehead and her gray hair. When he sat back up, he still held her hand in his lap. Her right hand, shaking slightly, moved gently down her chest. As Basil watched, and as Maggie observed from the doorway, Sacajawea slowly brought her beloved Jefferson Medal to her lips, kissing it warmly. She then placed the medal over her heart, with her hand covering it. Her eyes blinked more rapidly toward the ceiling, and she took a deep breath.

Then, without turning her head, she cast her eyes at Basil, as if silently asking his permission for something.

"Go back to sleep, mother," he said. "I will stay with you. I will always stay with you. And with the rise of the morning sun, you will be young again, and no longer tired. Just think of that day when you and Red caught those three fish."

Those were the last words Sacajawea heard, words that fittingly tied her to the Lewis and Clark Expedition, as did the Jefferson Medal that she still pressed to her heart. In her twilight years especially, according to her confidante Maggie, Sacajawea had constant dreams about the expedition and particularly her associations with William Clark, whom she came to think of as "Red."

"Thank you, son," Sacajawea said. "May you, when it is time, like me, go gentle into a peaceful night."

Those were the last words she ever spoke, words that would stay with Basil and Maggie for the rest of their days. They were totally sure that the last words Sacajawea spoke, and she spoke them clearly, were: *"May you, when it is time, like me, go gentle into a peaceful night."*

Her eyes — those very precious, ninety-six-year-old eyes — closed softly. Slowly, she drifted back to sleep, for the last time, as Basil still held her hand. He now also was softly humming.

At daybreak, Basil, with tears in his eyes, told Agent Lane and Reverend Roberts, "My mother is dead."

Later that same day — April ninth, 1884 — Basil and Reverend John Roberts buried Sacajawea on the Wind River Reservation in Wyoming, her final resting place.[157]

The End

EPILOGUE

This history of Sacajawea concludes with the bibliography section that includes exact renderings of the two documents frequently referenced in the text. They are Dr. Charles Eastman's ten-page report back to the U. S. Government in 1925 after his federally funded investigation into when and where Sacajawea died and where she is buried; and Reverend John Roberts' six-page statement in 1935, also requested by the U. S. Government, concerning the Shoshoni contention that he knew Sacajawea well and officiated at her burial on the Wind River in 1884.

The basic tenets of these two documents have stood the test of time and not only essentially corroborate each other but also validate the Traditional History of the Shoshones regarding Sacajawea's death and burial on April ninth, 1884, on the Wind River Reservation. The anti-Wyoming Sacajawea white historians — such as Ken Burns, Steven Ambrose and T. A. Larson — have to totally discredit these two documents in order to substantiate their claims that Sacajawea died in 1812 at Fort Manuel in South Dakota. In doing so, they are also discrediting two very respected and insightful men — Dr. Eastman and Reverend Roberts — as well as many other pillars of white and Shoshoni society, such as Sacajawea's fervently devoted, adopted son Basil. For example, to make the case that Sacajawea died in 1812, one would have to dismiss the fact that Basil was a significant force on the Wind River Reservation for decades leading right up to his cherished mother's death in 1884.

Dr. Eastman and Reverend Roberts were intelligent men with impeccable reputations, not to mention their topical insight that was totally beyond the scope of the anti-Wyoming Sacajawea revisionists. Their stark conclusions that Sacajawea died in 1884 on the Wind River Reservation in Wyoming, and is buried there, is supported by her own Shoshoni people, by the U. S. Government and by a myriad of other data from both the Indian and white worlds, as delineated in this book.

It is understandable, in the nineteenth century, that false sightings and little notes in the white world could fuel a controversy surrounding a celebrity of that period, especially when she traversed two cultures and societies as diverse as the white world and the Indian world. In modern times, for heaven's sake — even with contiguous television coverage saturating news events — the deaths of Elvis Pressley, John Kennedy, Princess Diana, Adolf Hitler, etc., still generate controversies and spawn continuous conspiracy theories. And those faces were known worldwide while few whites ever laid eyes on Sacajawea, and no one ever took her picture.

I feel the controversy concerning Sacajawea is uncalled for and not at all miniscule because, after all, she is the most memorialized female in America's long and storied history.

With the advent of yet another gigantic memorial to her — that heralded dollar coin stamped with the year 2000 — I think the time is ripe to end the Sacajawea controversy as to when and where she died and where she is buried.

Also, of course, with lavish plans already unfolding for the celebration of the Lewis and Clark bicentennial starting in 2003, that much more light will be shed on the Sacajawea legend, and rightfully so.

Thus, the dark cloud of controversy — however large it might be — should now be removed so the halos that Sacajawea deserves will glow that much more brightly. She did not die in South Dakota in 1812; she died in Wyoming in 1884.

Neither her gravesite nor the final seventy-two years of her very special life should ever be obliterated in the heritage of the America that she befriended so gracefully and so profoundly.

ENDNOTES

1 Boyer, Paul S.; Clark, Clifford, Jr.; etc.; The Enduring Vision: A History of the American People; Pages 170-172; Heath and Company Publishers; 1995.

2 Morley, Jacqueline. Across America: The Story of Lewis and Clark. (Watts, 1998).

3 Hebard, Dr. Grace; Sacajawea: A Guide and Interpreter of the Lewis and Clark Expedition. (Conyers Library Historicals, 1932).

4 Tarnese, John; Oral/Traditional History of the Shoshones; Audio Tape; Interview conducted by Rich Haney, 1995).

5 Burns, Ken; *WWW.pbs.org/Lewisandclark;* Internet, 1999.

6 Larson, T. A.; Wyoming: A History. (W. W. Norton & Company, 1977).

7 Clark, Ella; Edmonds, Margot. Sacagawea of the Lewis and Clark Expedition. (U. of Cal. Press, 1979).

8 Tarnese, John; Oral/Traditional History of the Shoshones; Audio Tape, 1995.

9 Allen, John Logan. Passage Through the Garden: Lewis and Clark and the Image of the American Northwest. Urbana: University of Illinois Press, 1995.

10 Tarnese, John. Oral/Traditional History of the Shoshones. Audio Tape, 1995.

11 Roberts, Philip. Wyoming Almanac. Page 205. Skyline West Press, 1989.

12 Schroer, Blanche. Sacajawea: The Legend and the Truth; In Wyoming magazine, 1977.

13 The Library of Congress, Washington, D. C. Article NA1076B. Internet www.loc.gov.

14 Tarnese, John. Oral/Traditional History of the Shoshones. Audio Tape, 1995.

15 DeVoto, Bernard. Journals of Lewis and Clark. Boston: Houghton Mifflin Co., 1953.

16 Tarnese, John. Oral/Traditional History of the Shoshones. Audio Tape, 1995.

17 Tarnese, John. Oral/Traditional History of the Shoshones. Audio Tape, 1995.

18 Large, Irtense. Sacajawea's Granddaughter Presents Paper On Her Famous Ancestor Before History Class at the University of Wyoming; July, 1926. Wyoming State Archives; Cheyenne, Wyoming.

19 Woodring, Minnie. Sacajawea's Story. Lander Journal; April 10, 1978.

20 Tarnese, John. Oral/Traditional History of the Shoshones. Audio Tape, 1995.

21 Waldo, Anna Lee.Sacajawea. Hearst Corporation Publishers; March, 1984.

22 Seymour, Flora. Sacajawea: American Pathfinder. Simon & Schuster Children's; March, 1991.

23 Boyer, Paul S. The Enduring Vision: A History of the American People. Heath and Company, 1995.

24 Hebard, Grace. Sacajawea: A Guide and Interpreter. Martino Publishing; Hardback Reprint, 1999.

25 Lewis, Meriwether. The Lewis and Clark Expedition. J. B. Lippincott Company. The 1814 Edition.

26 Hebard, Grace. Sacajawea: Guide of the Lewis and Clark Expedition. The Arthur H. Clark Co., 1932.

27 Rice, Deanna. Sacajawea, A Symposium. Annals of Wyoming; July , 1941; Vol. 13.

28 Eastman, Dr. Charles A. "Report to the U. S. Dept. of the Interior, Office of Indian Affairs." 1925.

29 The Library of Congress. *WWW.loc.gov.*, Article 19703. Internet listing, 1997.

30 Schroer, Blanche. Sacajawea: The Legend and the Truth. Wyoming State Archives, Cheyenne.

31 Larson, T. A. Wyoming: A History. W. W. Norton & Company, 1977.

32 Graff, Everrett D., Winnetka, Illinois. Holograph Letters to Blanche Schroer, Lander, WY.

33 Schroer, Blanche. Sacajawea: The Legend and the Truth. Wyoming State Archives, Cheyenne.

34 Tarnese, John. Oral/Traditional History of the Shoshones. Audio Tape, 1995.

35 DeVoto, Bernard. The Journals of Lewis and Clark. Houghton Mifflin Com., 1968.

36 Howard, Harold P. Sacajawea. University of Oklahoma Press, 1971.

37 Conlan, Roberta; Chief Editor. Indians of the Western Range. Time-Life Books, 1995; Page 86.

38 Lewis, Meriwether. The Lewis and Clark Expedition. J. B. Lippincott Company. The 1814 Edition.

39 Collyer, Bea. In the Footsteps of Lewis and Clark. National Geographic Society, 1970.

40 Tarnese, John. Oral/Traditional History of the Shoshones. Audio Tape, 1995.

41 Roberts, Reverend John. "Report to the U. S. Dept. of the Interior, Office of Indian Affairs;" 1935.

42 Tarnese, John. Oral/Traditional History of the Shoshones; Audio Tape, 1995.

43 Brackenridge, Henry M. "Journal of a Voyage up the Missouri, 1811." Arthur H. Clark Co, 1904.

44 Tarnese, John. Oral/Traditional History of the Shoshones. Audio Tape, 1995.

45 State Historical Society. 900 Governor's Drive; Pierre, South Dakota, 1999.

46 Lewis & Clark's Winter at Fort Mandan, 1804-1805; Lewis & Clark Interpretive Center; Washburn, ND.

47 Eastman, Dr. Charles A. "Report to the U. S. Dept. of the Interior, 1925."

48 Blumberg, Rhoda. The Incredible Journey of Lewis and Clark. Lothrop Publishing, 1987.

49 Lewis, Meriwether. The Lewis and Clark Expedition. J. B. Lippincott Company. The 1814 Edition.

50 People in the West: Sacajawea. *WWW.pbs.org/weta,* 1999.

51 Bergon, Frank. Original Journals of the Lewis and Clark Expedition (U. of Nebraska Press, 1983).

52 Tarnese, John. Oral/Traditional History of the Shoshones. Audio Tape, 1995.

53 Lewis, Meriwether. The Lewis and Clark Expedition. J. B. Lippincott Company. The 1814 Edition.

54 Ambrose, Steven E. Undaunted Courage (Simon & Schuster, 1996).

55 Conlan, Roberta; Managing Editor. Indians of the Western Range. (Time-Life Books, 1995).

56 Lewis, Meriwether; Clark, William. The History of the Lewis and Clark Expedition. Edited by Elliott Coues. (Dover Publications, 1994; reprint of 1893 edition).

57 Ogelsby, Richard Edward. The Opening of the Missouri Fur Trade. (U. of Oklahoma Press, 1964.)

58 Bergon, Frank. Original Journals of the Lewis and Clark Expedition. (Viking, 1989).

59 Stensland, Anna Lee. "Literature By and About the American Indian; An Annotated Bibliography." (Urbana, Illinois: National Council of Teachers of English, 1979).

60 Jassem, Jan. Sacajawea: Wilderness Guide. (New Library, 1979).

61 Papanek, John; Editor. The American Indians: The Woman's Way. (Time-Life Books, 1995).

62 Conlan, Roberta; Editor. Indians of the Western Range. (Time-Life Books, 1995).

63 Lewis, Meriwether. The Lewis and Clark Expedition. (J. B. Lippincott Company, 1814).

64 Tarnese, John. Oral/Traditional History of the Shoshones. (Audio Tape, 1995).

65 Shimkin, D. B. Wind River Shoshone Anthropological Records. (U. of Cal. Press, 1947).

66 Jackson, Donald. Letters of the Lewis and Clark Expedition. (U. of Illinois Press, 1962).

67 Lewis, Meriwether. The Lewis and Clark Expedition. (J. B. Lippincott Company, 1814).

68 Dietrich, Bill. "Explorer Lewis' Death Tied to Syphilis." (Special Report, The Seattle Times, 1995).

69 Hoxie, Frederick E. Encyclopedia of North American Indians. (Houghton Miflin Company, 1996).

70 Rowland, Della. The Story of Sacajawea. (Yearling Books, 1989).

71 PBS Online. Lewis and Clark: A timeline of the Trip. *WWW.pbs.org,* 1999.

72 Curry, Peggy. Sacajawea: Least Liberated. Casper Star-Tribune; March 28, 1976.

73 Fradin, Dennis. Sacajawea: The Journey to the West. (Library Binding, 1986).

74 Osgood, Ernest. The Field Notes of Captain William Clark, 1803-1805. (Yale U. Press, 1964).

75 Moulton, Gary. The Journals of the Lewis and Clark Expedition. (U. of Nebraska Press, 1988).

76 Dillon, Richard. Meriwether Lewis: A Biography. (Coward-McCanna of NY, 1965).

77 Conlan, Roberta; Managing Editor. Indians of the Western Range (Time-Life Books, 1995).

78 Large, Arlen. "Lewis and Clark Under Cover: We Proceeded On." (Vol. 15, #3; August, 1989).

79 Tarnese, John. Oral/Traditional History of the Shoshones; and Rowland, Della; The Story of Sacajawea. (Dell Yearling Biography, 1995).

80 Steffen, Jerome. William Clark: Jeffersonain Man on the Frontier. (U. of Oklahoma Press, 1977).

81 Dickinson, Norman. "The Enigmatic Sacajawea." (Published by the Fremont County Historical Society in Riverton, Wyoming, 1975).

82 Woodring, Minnie. Sacajawea's Story. (Reprint, Lander Journal; April 10, 1978).

83 Tarnese, John. Oral/Traditional History of the Shoshones; and Woodring, Minnie; Sacajawea's Story.

84 Twitchell, Bernice; Horne, Esther; daughters of Sacajawea intimate F. G. Burnett in co-written statement registered in 1978 and presented to Wyoming State Archives, Cheyenne, Wyoming.

85 Horne, Esther. Our Wind River Sacajawea. Lander Journal, 1979.

86 Bartlett, Ichabod S. History of Wyoming. (S. J. Clarke Publishing Company, 1918).

87 Clarke, Charles G. The Men of the Lewis and Clark Expedition. (Arthur Clark Company, Pub., 1970).

88 Hoxie, Frederick E. Encyclopedia of North American Indians. (Houghton Miflin Company, 1996).

89 Hebard, Grace. Washakie: Chief of the Shoshones. (Clark Company Pub., 1918).

90 Documents/Statements/Research by Hebard, Dr. Grace; Tarnese, John; Eastman, Dr. Charles; Roberts, Reverend John, etc., etc.

91 Schroer, Blanche. Sacajawea: The Legend and the Truth. (Wyoming State Archives, Cheyenne).

92 Dickinson, Norman. The Enigmatic Sacajawea. Wyoming State Archives, Cheyenne; 1975.

93 Tarnese, John. The Oral/Traditional History of the Shoshones. Audio Tape, 1995.

94 Siebert, David Roger. "A History of the Shoshone Indians of Wyoming." (U. of WYO archives, 1961).

95 Hultkranz, Ake. "The Shoshones of the Rocky Mountain Area." (Annals of Wyoming, 1961, Vol. 33).

96 Curry, Peggy. Sacajawea: Least Liberated. (Casper Star-Tribune;

March 29, 1976).

97 Conlan, Roberta: Chief Editor. Indians of the Western Range. (Time-Life Books, 1995).

98 PBS Online. (WWW.pbs.org/Lewisandclark/archive/source.html).

99 Steffen, Jerome. William Clark: Jeffersonian Man on the Frontier. (U. of Oklahoma Press, 1977).

100 Ambrose, Stephen. Undaunted Courage. (Simon & Schuster, 1996).

101 Betts, Robert. In Search of York: The Slave with Lewis and Clark. (U. of Colorado Press, 1985).

102 Ambrose, Stephen. (PBS Online: Lewis and Clark; *WWW.pbs.org/lewis* andclark/archive).

103 PBS Online. Lewis and Clark: The Archive. (WWW.pbs.org/Lewisandclark/archive/source.html).

104 DeVoto, Bernard. Journals of Lewis and Clark. (Boston: Houghton Mifflin Co., 1953).

105 Clarke, Charles. The Men of the Lewis & Clark Expedition. (Arthur H. Clark Company, CA, 1970).

106 Chuinard, Eldon. Only One Man Died. (The Arthur H. Clark Co., Glendale, CA, 1979).

107 Lavender, David. The Way to the Western Sea. (New York: Harper & Row, 1988).

108 Ronda, James P. Lewis and Clark Among the Indians. (Lincoln: U. of Nebraska Press, 1984).

109 Appleman, Roy E. Lewis and Clark: Historic Places. (U. S. Department of the Interior, 1975).

110 Anderson, Irving W. "A Charbonneau Family Portrait." (Fort Clatsop Historical Association, 1998).

111 Clark, Helen. "Where Is the Grave of Sacajawea?" (Near West Magazine, Vol. 10, 1967).

112 "Sacajawea: A Symposium." (Annals of Wyoming, Vol. 13, 1941).

113 Tarnese, John. Oral/Traditional History of the Shoshones. (Audio Tape, 1995).

114 Hebard, Grace. Sacajawea of the Lewis and Clark Expedition. (Conyers Historicals, 1932).

115 Chapman, Abraham. "A Gathering of Indian Memories." (New American Library, 1975).

116 Pike, Ella. "Shoshones in Wind River Area of Wyoming." (National Anthropological Archives, Washington, D. C.).

117 Tarnese, John. Oral/Traditional History of the Shoshones. (Audio Tape, 1995).

118 Eastman, Dr. Charles. "Report to the Dept. of Interior, 1925." (National Archives, Wash., D. C.).

119 "Census Roll of the Shoshone Tribe." (Wyoming State Archives, Cheyenne, 1984).

120 Large, Irtense. "Papers of Sacajawea's Granddaughter." (Wyoming State Archives, Cheyenne, 1926).

121 Tarnese, John. The Oral/Traditional History of the Shoshones. (Audio Tape, 1995).

122 Clark, Helen. "Where Is the Grave of Sacajawea?" (Near West Magazine, Vol. 10, 1967).

123 Large, Irtense. "Sacajawea's Granddaughter's Papers." (Wyoming State Archives, 1926); and Tarnese, John. Oral/Traditional History of the Shoshones. (Audio Tape, 1995).

124 Dykes, Jim. "A Trail of Tears." (Parade Magazine, Sunday Supplement Nationally, 1989).

125 Hoxie, Frederick E. Encyclopedia of North American Indians. (Houghton Miflin Company, 1996).

126 Oko, Dan. "Indian Saved Lewis and Clark." (Associated Press, Missoula, Montana; July 6, 1999).

127 Wiget, Andrew. Dictionary of Native American Literature. (Garland Publishing, 1994).

128 Stensland, Anna. Literature By and About the American Indians. (National Teachers Council, 1979).

129 Brown, Dee. Bury My Heart at Wounded Knee. (Holt, Rinehart and Winston Publishers, 1970).

130 Eastman, Charles. "Report to the Dept. of the Interior, 1925." (National Archives, Wash., D. C.).

131 Roberts, Reverend John. "Report to the Department of the Interior, Office of Indian Affairs, 1935." (National Archives, Wash., D. C.).

132 Eastman, Charles. "Report to the U. S. Dept. of the Interior, 1925." (National Archives, Wash. D. C.).

133 Dykes, Jim. "A Trail of Tears." (Parade Magazine, 1989); and Deloria, Vine, Jr. Behind the Trail of Broken Treaties. (Delacorte Press/New York, 1974).

134 Tarnese, John. Oral/Traditional History of the Shoshones. (Audio Tape, 1995).

135 Brady, C. T. Recollections of a Missionary in the Great West. (Charles Scribners' Son, NY; 1900).

136 Clark, Helen. Sacajawea. Near West magazine; May, 1967. (Wyoming State Archives, Cheyenne).

137 Hunter, Bonnie. These Americans in Moccasins. (Library Binding, 1977).

138 Schroer, Blanche. Sacajawea: The Legend and the Truth. (1977, Wyoming State Archives, Cheyenne).

139 WWW.pbs.org/Lewisandclark/Sacajaweasearchbio.

140 Traditional History of the Shoshones; private research of Dr. Grace Hebard; governmental research of Dr. Charles Eastman; etc., etc.

141 Tarnese, John. Oral/Traditional History of the Shoshones. (Audio Tape, 1995).

142 Boyer, Paul. The Enduring Vision: A History of the American People (Heath & Company, 1995).

143 DeVoto, Bernard. The Course of Empire. (Houghton Miffliln Company, 1952).

144 Farb, Peter. Man's Rise to Civilization as Shown by the Indians of North America. (E. P. Dutton & Company, Inc., 1968 Hardback and 1989 Library Binding Softback reprint).

145 Dykes, Jim. A Trail of Tears. Atlanta Weekly Magazine; December 15, 1985.

146 Tarnese, John. Oral/Traditional History of the Shoshones. (Audio Tape, 1995).

147 Annual Reports. U. S. Commissioner of Indian Affairs, 1860-1891.

148 Annual Reports. U. S. Bureau of American/Indian Ethnology, 10th Report; and U. S. Commissioner of Indian Affairs; Annual Reports, 1860-1891.

149 The Library of Congress, Washington, D. C. (*WWW.loc.gov,* 1999).

150 Morris, Glenn. "The Assault on the Dann Ranch." (NEA Syndicated Newspaper Column, 1993).

151 The Library of Congress. (*WWW.loc.gov,* 1999).

152 Tarnese, John. Oral/Tradition History of the Shoshones. (Audio Tape, 1995).

153 Tarnese, John. Oral/Traditional History of the Shoshones. (Audio Tape, 1995).

154 Dye, Eva Emery. The Conquest. (Thompson & Son Publishers; California Imprint, 1902).

155 Brown, Mark H. The Plainsman of the Yellowstone. (New York: Putnam's, 1961).

156 Woodring, Minnie. "Sacajawea's Story." (Lander Journal, April 10, 1978).

157 Tarnese, John. Oral/Traditional History of the Shoshones. Audio Tape, 1995; original tape donated to Wyoming State Archives, Barrett Building, Cheyenne, Wyoming, 1999).

BIBLIOGRAPHY

(In addition to the 157 endnotes, general reference material was also utilized from these sources).

Schanzer, Rosalyn. How We Crossed the West: The Adventures of Lewis and Clark (The National Geographic Society, 1997).

Ambrose, S. E. Undaunted Courage (Simon & Schuster, 1996).

Morley, Jacqueline. Across America: The Story of Lewis and Clark (Watts, 1998).

Bergon, Frank, ed. Original Journals of the Lewis and Clark Expedition. (Viking, 1989).

Moulton, G. E., ed. Atlas of the Lewis and Clark Expedition (U. of Nebraska Press, 1983).

Satterfield, Archie. The Lewis and Clark Trail (Stackkpole, 1978).

Stuart, Granville. Forty Years on the Frontier. (Arthur H. Clark Company, 1925).

Hebard, Dr. Grace. Sacajawea. (Conyers Library Historicals, 1904).

Deloria, Jr., Vine. Behind the Trail of Broken Treaties (Delacorte Press, 1974).

Maxfield, R. D. Wyoming: A Guide to Historic Sites. Pages 86-87. (Big Horn Pub., 1976).

Brown, Dee. Bury My Heart at Wounded Knee. (Holt, Rinehart & Winston, 1970).

Boyer, Paul S.; Clark, Clifford E., etc.; The Enduring Vision. (Heath & Company, 1995).

Conlan, Roberta; Managing Ed. Indians of the Western Range (Time-Life Books, 1995).

Conlan, Roberta; Managing Editor. War for the Plains. (Time-Life Books, 1994).

Roberts, Philip J. Wyoming Almanac. (Skyline West Press, 1989).

Urbanek, Mae. Wyoming Place Names. (Johnson Publishing Company, 1974).

Sodaro, Craig; Adams, Randy. Frontier Spirit: Story of Wyoming. (Johnson Books, 1986).

Larson, T. A. Wyoming: A History. (W. W. Norton & Company, 1977).

Lewis, Meriwether. The Lewis and Clark Expedition. (J. B. Lippincott Company, 1814).

Howard, Major General Otis O. Famous Indian Chiefs I've Known (Century Pub., 1908).

Blumberg, Rhoda. The Incredible Journey of Lewis and Clark (Lothrop, 1987).

Clark, Ella E.; Edmonds, Margot. Sacagawea of the Lewis and Clark Expedition (U. of California Press, 1979).

Lewis, Meriwether; Clark, William. The History of the Lewis and Clark Expedition (Edited By Elliott Coues; Dover Publications, 1994; reprint of 1893 edition).

Documents/Articles/Tapes

Eastman, Dr. Charles; ten-page statement to the U. S. Government in 1925.

Roberts, Reverend John; six-page statement to U. S. Government in 1935.

Morris, Glenn; 1993 NEA syndicated newspaper column on The Treaty of Ruby Valley and The Assault on the Dann Ranch.

Bowman, Sally-Jo; From Where the Sun Now Stands; National Parks Magazine, January/February, 1999.

Tarnese, John; Oral/Traditional History of the Shoshones; three audio tapes of Interview with Shoshoni Elder conducted by Rich Haney, 1995.

***

Note: In 1924 the United States Government recognized that Sacajawea, the Shoshoni girl that was the heroine of the 1805—06 Lewis and Clark Expedition, had become a figure of vast historical importance. Yet, some statues, monuments, memorials, books and newspaper articles said she died in 1812 in South Dakota while others maintained she died in 1884 in Wyoming. Congress thus funded an investigation and named a highly respected Indian expert, Dr. Charles Eastman, to lead that investigation. He was commissioned to report back to the government as to when and where Sacajawea died and where she was buried. What follows is an exact word-for-word copy of Dr. Eastman's ten-page, typed report to the United States Government, minus a plethora of documents and exhibits he included to buttress his findings. The punctuation and style precisely replicates Dr. Eastman.

***

United States
DEPARTMENT OF THE INTERIOR
Office of Indian Affairs
Washington

March 2, 1925

The Commissioner of Indian Affairs.

My dear Mr. Commissioner:

In pursuance of your instructions of December 13, 1924, relative to the investigation and locating the final burial place of Sacajawea or Bird Woman, I enter upon the investigation by the first of January, 1925. As by instructions, I proceeded from Pawhuska, Oklahoma, to Fort Washakie, Wyoming. I fully realized the importance and delicacy of this investigation, therefore I secured special interpreters before I entered upon the work. Mr. James E. Compton, who understood not only the Shoshone language but the Bannocks and he is a well-educated Carlisle man, not only this but is well versed in the modern history of his people.

Mr. R. P. Haas, the local superintendent, gave every help possible to find and meet such persons as I thought would give any material evidence concerning "Bazile's mother" as she was commonly known in her later days, although she was also known as Porivo, Chief Woman. She was also known by the name of Wadziwiper and Pohaniv or Grass Woman. Wadziwiper means Lost Woman, who claims to be or others claim for her that she is Sacajawea or Bird Woman, the interpreter and guide of the Lewis and Clark Expedition.

I will use the Shoshone or Comanche name Porivo for convenience. This statement of her grandson, Andrew Bazile, I marked as Exhibit A establishes fully that Porivo is the mother of Bazile and Baptiste, two well-known Shoshone men; all died within three years, namely: Porivo died 1884; Bazile died in 1886; and Baptiste died in 1885. At the best information I have she was very nearly 100 years of age. If she is Sacajawea or Bird Woman she must have been born in 1788, and according to Lewis and Clark journals she would be 96 years old when she died. If Baptiste, the son of Porivo, is the same Baptiste, the son of Sacajawea, he would have been 80 years old when he died for he was born February 11, 1805, according to Lewis and Clark journals; and if Bazile, the son of Porivo, is the same as Touisant Charbonneau, the child of Charbonneau's Snake wife whose name is Otter Woman.

According to the Gros Ventres testimony, he would be 83 years old, since in Luttig's application for guardianship for him in August, 1813, he was declared 10 years old. This would make him approximately 1-1/2 to 2 years older than his brother, Baptiste. These were the essential points I set down to guide me in the investigation.

It is well know in history that when Lewis and Clark returned from the western coast they lingered for a short time at the Gros Ventres village, and it is well known that Charbonneau and his two Snake wives remained there when Lewis and Clark's Expedition proceeded down the river to St. Louis.

The Indians of the Fort Berthold Reservation, North Dakota, insisted that he did not pick up these Snake wives at the village and afterwards marry them, but they insisted he had married them somewhere up the Missouri River, either among the Crow Indians or the Blackfeet and afterwards drifted to their country and was there only a short time when Lewis and Clark's Expedition came up to their village. It is very evident and in accordance with the customs of the Indians that Charbonneau could not have married the two girls at the same time. He must have married one of them at least a year or possibly two years before he married the second wife. To be sure he kept both of them, Touisant Charbonneau being the child of his first Shoshone wife, namely Otter Woman, and this wife must have been his favorite for he named his oldest daughter Otter Woman, of the Gros Ventres wife by the name of Eagle, nearly twelve years afterwards, who was the mother of Bull Eye's, who now claims that his grandmother Eagle was Sacajawea.

According to the satement of Mrs. Weidemann, a very intelligent woman, daughter of Great Chief Poor Wolf of the Hidatsa Indians, Charbonneau took both of his wives and their children down to St. Louis; a year or so afterwards Lewis and Clark departed from the village to St. Louis. I submit Mrs. Weidemann's statement as Exhibit K.

The writings of Miss Stella G. Drumm of the St. Louis Historical Society say that after they reached St. Louis and remained for a short time Charbonneau was hired out to the fur company of Chouteau and was sent to one of their forts in the southwest. It is not clear as to what trading post he was attached, but it was on the branches of the Red River or Arkansas River in Oklahoma. However, he returned to St. Louis before 1811 for he had sold what little property he had in St. Louis to William Clark for $100.

In Breckenridge's Book of Travels he states that in 1811 when he was coming up the Missouri River on boats he saw Touisant Charbonneau and his Snake wife. He was told that the Frenchman was the guide of the Lewis and Clark Expedition. He also spoke of his wife as imitating white women's style in dressing and he spoke of her as being a commendable woman. In 1813 Manuel Lisa, a well-known French fur trader at St. Louis, whose operations in the fur trading business was extensive, had sent a large body of men up the river to establish a trading post on the Missouri River in the vicinity of the then Arikiras and Gros Ventres as well as Yankton Nais Sioux country. John Luttig was his chief clerk who kept a daily Journal apparently of the activities and experiences of the party and the fort. On September 18, 1812, he made an entry saying "Elie's Snake squaw died today." On December 20, 1812, another entry was made by Luttig, saying "Charbonneau's wife, the Snake squaw, died of Putrid fever, the best woman in the fort." The people of the fort had a great deal of trouble from the Indians of the region owing to the American-English War of 1812, during which some of the British traders were inciting the Indians against the Americans. During the winter according to Luttig's Journal that Charbonneau and Jessiumme were suspected seriously of being involved in the hostile conduct of some of the Indians. Luttig's Journal stopped suddenly in March, 1813. It is well known among the Indians, Sioux and Rees, that that fort was attacked during that time and killed many of Lisa's men. It appears during that time Charbonneau had departed to Gros Ventres country.

In August, 1813, Luttig made an application at the Orphan Court in St. Louis to have guardians appointed for the children of Touisant Charbonneau deceased, to wit:

> Touisant Charbonneau, a boy 10 years of age.
> Lizette Charbonneau, a baby girl, 1 year of age.

It appears or can be inferred that when the trouble arose at Fort Manuel Charbonneau had left his children, presumably in the care of the Indian wives of the other employees of the fort, when his wife died December 20, and as he disappeared during the attack there, the children were brought down with the remainder of the party to St. Louis.

John Luttig, in his Journal, expressed himself strongly against the character of Charbonneau, but he spoke of his Shoshone wife as being the best woman in the fort. He took interest in these children of the Charbonneau woman. He saw to it that they should have a guardian, therefore William Clark was appointed. And apparently he supposed that Charbonneau had been killed in the outbreak at the fort.

In the three points, Dr. Robinson holds as the essential proof that the woman who died on December 20 is the Bird Woman. I find no place in this connection where her name Sacajawea was mentioned nor directly referred to as Sacajawea, except in Mr. Breckenridge's observation on the boat that Charbonneau was pointed out as guide for Lewis and Clark.

That he had a Shoshone wife with him whom he naturally supposed was the one that accompanied Charbonneau across the continent with the Lewis and Clark Expedition. It is apparent that the Bird Woman was not called Sacajawea as far as the public is concerned during this time. Up to this time Sergt. Patrick Gass's journal was the only one published in 1807. No where in his report was she called Sacajawea; she was only referred to as the squaw or Charbonneau's wife.

After the revision of the Lewis and Clark Journals no one knew at that time outside of Lewis and Clark and Charbonneau that this woman was called Sacajawea. Secondly, the court record shows that Baptiste, the child of Sacajawea, was conspicuously absent; this means that Baptiste had been retained in St. Louis when Charbonneau and his other Snake wife and child had gone back to the Indian country as stated by Breckenridge. Baptiste was too young to be separated from his mother and in my knowledge of the Indian mothers' traits and habits are such she could not have permitted to be separated from her child at that age, especially those times. It was hard enough thirty years ago to get a child of 10 years to leave their Indian parents to go to school. It would have been impossible for Clark to retain Baptiste without his mother, but as he determined to either adopt or educate the boy, the youngest member of the expedition across the continent, he had to provide for the Bird Woman in order to keep Baptiste in St. Louis so that he may see to his education and as he could not trust Touisant Charbonneau to take the child back up the Missouri; therefore he retains him and that is why Baptiste was not mentioned in the Orphans Court when Luttig applied for guardian to be selected, or appointed, for the children of Touisant Charbonneau, deceased on August, 1813.

The evidence given by Wolfe Chief or the Hidatsa and Mrs. Weidemann shows that Charbonneau did have two Shoshone wives and a Mandan wife besides. They clearly stated that Charbonneau took both of his Shoshone wives with him when he visited St. Louis some time in 1907 to 1808 and it is evident that he had returned with but one Shoshone wife who died on December 20, 1812. In the St. Louis court applications for guardians for his children, the child of Bird Woman was conspicuously absent. It will seem then that this child had been left in St. Louis when Charbonneau returned north in 1811, but the child Baptiste would have been too young to be separated from his mother, the Bird Woman.

When the other two children of Charbonneau — namely, Touisant Charbonneau, Jr., and Lizette Charbonneau, daughter — were presented at the Orphans Court, John Luttig was appointed guardian but it was scratched off and substituted by William Clark.

Miss Stella E. Drumm states in her book that Clark was absent at the time of the court procedure, but when he returned he accepted the guardianship of the other children of Charbonneau. It is natural for the Indian woman, and under the circumstances, that she would have to become the mother of those children until a certain age when they can be sent to school. This is proven by the testimony of Eagle Woman and by the statement of Mrs. Weidemann when Charbonneau married the bride, Eagle, Hidatsa maiden, in 1819 or 1820. He proceeded immediately with a company of fur traders to St. Louis, although he was supposed to have been killed in the attack at Fort Manuel by the Sioux when they killed many of Lisa's men. He turned up unexpectedly at St. Louis with his new wife, Eagle, and he takes his old wife again, Bird Woman, and the two boys Baptiste and Bazile.

Apparently Touisant Charbonneau, Jr., had a name of his own by that time, namely, Bazile. These two boys had been educated by Willliam Clark; one was sent to a Protestant missionary teacher and the other was sent to a Catholic missionary teacher, namely, Mr. Welch and Father Neil, until in 1820. Bazile must have been 17 years old and Baptiste 15.

Eagle said they were about 18 and 15. Not more than a year or so remaining in St. Louis according to Mrs. Weidemann's statement and Eagle's own account that Charbonneau had obtained employment with one of the fur companies together with his sons and the whole family departs for the southwest. They worked as guides and interpreters in one or two forts in the neighborhood of Neosho and Washita Rivers. During that time they visited some other forts, among them some Spanish or Mexican trading posts where Eagle gives account of seeing "so many sea shells and beads and beautiful blankets." While they were in that part of the country (it appears to be the western part of Oklahoma and Kansas), when Charbonneau takes another wife, namely a Ute young woman, which causes trouble with the Bird Woman. Charbonneau whips Bird Woman during the absence of his two sons on a trip. The Bird Woman disappears. This statement is corroborated by the statement of Bazile's son, namely Andrew Bazile, Exhibit A. Afterwards she drifted among the Comanches. The Comanches were originally a part of the Shoshone Nation; they spoke the same language with a dialect and local differences, just like we say high and low Dutch language.

The evidences of the Comanches, or rather the statements of the Comanches people, bear out this fact although there is no one now living who knew just how and when she appeared among them. In due time she married a man by the name of Jirk Meat from whom she had 5 children. All died in infancy except one son and the youngest child, a girl. She lived approximately 26 or 27 years among the Comanches when her husband, Jirk Meat, was killed in battle. It is a fact this was the first husband of her own choice and apparently she was devoted to him, therefore at his death she was heartbroken and very much depressed. At that time she was not in harmony with the relatives of her husband, therefore she declared she would not live among them any longer. When she said this she disappeared, taking with her her little girl. She had in her family a Mexican captive girl whom her son had captured in war and Bird Woman had raised her. She was 15 years old. She gives the information that Bird Woman had taken a small parflesche bag containing dried buffalo meat. It appears from this that she had a definite purpose and point toward which she was going.

Her son hunted for her everywhere; in fact her whole band searched for her in vain. He visited many of the adjacent tribes, namely, Wichitas and Kiowas, but she was not found. A rumor came to them that she was among the white people; whether this was true or not they did not know. She was gone forever. After this they called her Wadzewiper, the Lost Woman. During her life with the Comanches she was called Porivo, which means Wife or Chief Woman. Nothing was ever heard concerning her until the Indians all were placed in reservations and schools were established. Carlisle also came into existence. The son that she left among the Comanches was called Ticannaf. He had three or four children, all dead except one living now, a woman whose name is Tahcutine who gave the story of the life of her grandmother or Porivo or Sacajawea, the Bird Woman. The great grandchild from the Comanches and the great grandchildren from the Shoshones met at Carlisle. They inquired of each other their great grandmother's descendants, which developed that they were many living among the two tribes at the present time, and for the first time they learned that Porivo had reached her tribe the Shoshones, some fifty years after she disappeared from the Comanches. This story of her life as given by the

Comanche descendants confirms the testimony of the Shoshones; that when she returned to her tribe she told them that she came from the Comanches, although it took her several years to reach there.

The story of her separation from her husband and her children is corroborated by the statement of Andrew Bazile, a grandchild and the son of Bazile, saying that his father told him that the Bird Woman and her husband separated in the southwest country when he and his brother were young men and they have never seen their father since. They only saw their mother when she came back to them at Fort Bridger, a gray haired woman. The next place where she appeared was in the testimony of Edmond LeClair in Exhibit C.

The story of Sally Ann, who accompanied the Bird Woman or Porivo from Portage, the Sioux position is given fully by this witness, namely, Edmond LeClair. She reached St. Louis somehow a year or two after she disappeared from the Comanches and remained perhaps a year or so at that place, then proceeded up the Missouri River with some of the river fur men. At this time she married an old Frenchman who was employed by the company; the name of this man was not given.

Information came to me indirectly from the Sioux country along the Missouri River that the Bird Woman is know 70 years ago, but the testimony of Wolfe Chief or the Hidatsa and Mrs. Weidemann shows that she had passed up the Missouri River stopping at the various forts until she reached Fort Union at the mouth of Yellowstone River. It does not clearly state how many years she traveled up the Missouri River or how many years she remained at Fort Union, but the story is clear that she proceeded from Fort Union up the Yellowstone River, Big Horn and Wind Rivers in company with French Indian traders who were sent out from Fort Union to trade with the Rocky Mountain Indians. This story is that her husband was left behind for a few days at Fort Union with the intention of joining the party at the mouth of Big Horn River, but he never appeared. It was supposed he might have been killed by some Indian war party. Thus she lost her husband. On this trip she succeeded in reaching the upper branches of the Snake River when she learned from her tribe, some of who she met, that her two sons were at Fort Bridger. She worked her way south until she reached Fort Bridger where she found her two sons. The family reunion was natural and a happy one. Bazile, the oldest son, or her step son whom she raised and called her own son, was exceptionally devoted to her. It was in his family that she lived and died.

The testimony of Mr. F. G. Burnette, Edmond LeClair, and Andrew Bazile corroborate Porivo's traveling from Fort Union to the Snake country. Porivo's life among the Comanches is proved by the testimony of Mrs. Weidemann and the story of Eagle Charbonneau. Hidatsa wife and Andrew Bazile proves the separation of Charbonneau and Bird Woman in the vicinity of the Comanche country which identifies that the Bird Woman and Porivo are the same person, and that Bazile and Baptiste were sons of Porivo or the sons of the Bird Woman. Bazile was not a real son but was a step son whom she raised as her own son. There are many instances among the Indians where a nephew or step son has been more devoted to the mother than the real son. This was the case in the relation of Bazile and his mother.

The Shoshone woman who died at Fort Manuel was Otter Woman, the other Shoshone wife of Charbonneau who was Bazile's mother. The child (girl) Lazette does not appear anywhere after the court procedure. It is likely she died in childhood. The child that Porivo or Bird Woman carried away from the Comanche tribe had reached womanhood among the Shoshone people and married a Frenchman by the name of Ely Mayer, who left and went to California; then she married Shade Large. She died soon after without any issue. The testimonies concerning this woman are not taken in due form as I did not think it was pertinent to the investigation of the burying place of Sacajawea.

In the testimony of Mrs. Weidemann and Eagle tells the story of her trip with Charbonneau to St. Louis and the southwest, and after the break with Bird Woman they joined another large party of fur traders who proceeded to Salt Lake in which Charbonneau was employed, taking with him his Ute wife and the Hidatsa wife, but after winter quarters had broken up, they decided to proceed northeast into the Wind River country. The Ute wife left him. They then proceeded over the mountains towards the Wind River. When they reached that point they followed down the Big Horn River, thence to the Yellowstone River. When they were in this vicinity they met a large body of Crow Indians in camp. Here Eagle found some relatives who gave a white horse to Charbonneau. They proceeded down the Yellowstone River until they reached the Missouri River and down that river they arrived at the Hidatsa village where they had left four or five years before, when they went down to St. Louis. This was about 1825 when they arrived at the village of Hidatsa.

It was on the basis of this wonderful trip that her grandson, Bull Eye's, makes the claim that his grandmother was the Bird Woman who accompanied Lewis and Clalrk, but it was fully 15 years later that this trip was made as the statement of his own tribeswoman and Mrs. Weidemann who clears the case, and in the part of his own statement that it was an entirely different trip.

It is also apparent that Charbonneau considered his Shoshone wife, Otter Woman, was his favorite for he named the first child by his wife, Eagle, the same name, namely, Otter the mother of Bull Eye's. The evidences gathered by Dr. Grace Raymond Hebard is authentic because it came from the Bird Woman at the time; although she was an old woman then, she spoke of the incidences on the Lewis and Clark Expedition. At the time history was unknown to even some of the Rocky Mountain white men, much more so with the Indians. One of the striking characteristics and habits of the Bird Woman is that she is very modest in claiming any honors of being guide to that party; one reason for this is the Indian women will put her husband as the head in any matter of that kind. She never considered herself as a guide or interpreter. She evidently assumed that the great duties performed by her were the natural consequences of the expedition; that she was not interpreter and guide as she did not receive any salary and it will not bear too much assumption to say that she did not consider herself important or noted until perhaps some time after; even then she could not have received any published statement about herself as her people were very illiterate at the time of her death; and, as regards to her silence about her wonderful traveling and career, because it was not her choice but fate seemed to have compelled her to live the life that she did, except when she married the Comanche man. She was then a real wife and happy with her husband. Therefore when he was killed she was heartbroken and dissatisfied with the tribe with whom she lived and again the thought of her nativity and tribe took strong hold of her, therefore she departed with her youngest child on her back. Her purpose was clearly defined for she carried it out and in the end she defeated fate.

Within a short time that I am allotted to investigate and locate the burial place of this woman, it was difficult for me to go into all the trails and evidences of her wanderings, but I have only gone to the important points where she actually lived and the tradition still exists of her being there, and follow her back to her nation as hereintofore stated. She died April 9, 1884, and was buried by Missionary Roberts at Fort Washakie, Wyoming.

Not only the identity of Sacajawea, the Bird Woman, is proven by the accompanying testimonies taken in the very wide parts of the country in such a manner that they could not have known what the other tribes knew and still they corroborated the truth of the history of her travels.

Porivo or Chief Woman and Sacajawea, the Bird Woman, are one and the same person.

Bazile and Baptiste, the sons of Porivo or Sacajawea, are the same sons of Touisant Charbonneau's wife, Sacajawea or the Bird Woman of the Lewis and Clark Expedition, namely, Touisant Charbonneau, Jr., and Baptiste Charbonneau. This is proven by the statement of Mrs. Weidemann of the story of Eagle's trip with Charbonneau to St. Louis, southwestern territory and through Salt

Lake country; thence back by the way of Wind, Big Horn, and Yellowstone Rivers into the Missouri and back to the Gros Ventres village reaching there about 1825.

Charbonneau was absent from that part of the country between 1819 and 1825, after which he was seen in that part of the country again by the Government officials, Atkinson and O'Fallon. From there on he was seen by Prince Maximillian, Mr. Larpenteur, and others up to 1839 when he appeared in St. Louis and he has never been seen since.

By the testimonies gathered by Dr. Grace Raymond Hebard, Baptiste was seen among the trappers in the Lemhi country in 1830. Faris speaks of having been lost in the trapping trip for two or three days, but he appeared later.

William Clark Kernley spoke of meeting him in 1843 in the vicinity of Fort Laramie, Wyoming, as a guide, and Fremont in his exploring trip across to the Pacific meets a body of employees of the fur traders, Bent and St. Vraine, not far from Fort St. Vraine on the south fork of the Platte in a camp which was managed by Charbonneau.

It is stated in Jim Faris' account of a trapping party in which Bazile Charbonneau and his brother were employed by Bent and Robideau at Bent's forts in the southwest on some branches of the Arkansas. Bent and St. Vraine later on opened forts on the south forks of the Platte River and sent their men into the recesses of the mountains for trapping and gathering furs from different Indian tribes.

It is natural that these two men being employed by that fur company wandered up into that country which was approximately adjacent to the country of their ancestors, namely, the Snake Indians to which their mother was a member, namely Bird Woman. Evidently the older one took upon himself the leadership of the uncle's tribe at the same time he was still serving Robideau, Bent, St. Vraine, and later Jim Bridger.

What evidence Dr. Hebard gathered came from very competent people, both intelligent and strong men.

The testimony of Drs. Erwin, Patten, and Roberts can not

easily be disputed. In the first place they were simple men; secondly, they were Christian men for all three of them were missionaries at different times or simultaneously in which they were engaged in work among the Indians, and all of them had known Porivo, Bazille's mother or Sacajawea, the Bird Woman.

Sacajawea, the Bird Woman, was not much older than her sons. She was 17 when she gave birth to her son, Baptiste. Bazile or Touisant Charbonneau, Jr., the son of Otter Woman, the other Snake wife of Charbonneau, was born nearly two years before Baptiste. Therefore he was only 15 years younger than the Bird Woman. At the time their mother died they were very old men, she being 96 years old. Not knowing the exact age the Indians said she was about 100 years of age. Baptiste was 80 years old and Bazile was 83. Therefore they did not appear much younger at that age than their mother and they all died within three years.

I submit the testimonies of three different Indian nations, namely, Shoshones, Comanches, and Gros Ventres, the first in Wyoming, the second in Oklahoma, and the third in North Dakota. As there were no authentic records to be found after Clark had finished with them, Bird Woman and sons, we have to accept the tribal traditions and when they corroborated so strikingly well, we must accept it as the truth.

I report that Sacajawea, after sixty years of wandering from her own tribe, returns to her people at Fort Bridger and lived the remainder of her life with her sons in peace until she died on April 9, 1884, at Fort Washakie, Wyoming, that is her final resting place.

Respectfully,
Chas. A. Eastman,
Inspector and Investigator

Note: By 1935, Sacajawea had emerged as the most memorialized female in American history. And yet, some historians were still saying she died in 1812 in South Dakota while others maintained she died in 1884 in Wyoming. Thus, there was no consensus as to when and where she was buried. Some members of Congress thought this was ridiculous when a statue in one town would register her 1812 death while a statue in the next town would list her death as having occurred in 1884. John Roberts, the young minister that supposedly knew Sacajawea well and officiated at her burial in 1884 on the Wind River Reservation in Wyoming, was still alive. The U. S. Government asked for his official statement, wanting it in its archives before he died. Here is the six-page document, word-for-word and unedited, that the elderly but still very alert Reverend Roberts provided to the U. S. Government on April first, 1935.

***

OFFICE OF INDIAN AFFAIRS, WASHINGTON, D. C.

April 1, 1935
The Death of Sacajawea
By John Roberts, D. D., L. L. D.

Much has been written of the achievements of Sacajawea, the Shoshone girl who guided the Lewis and Clark expedition across the Northwest Territory to the Pacific. The Reverend John Roberts, Protestant Episcopal Missionary at the Shoshone Agency, now sends us this account of her death.

The Right Reverend John F. Spalding, Bishop of the missionary jurisdiction of Colorado and Wyoming, sent me here in 1883 to establish the Shoshone and Arapahoe Indian mission of the Protestant Episcopal Church. I arrived at the Shoshone Agency on February tenth after a hard journey over the main range of the Rockies from Green River, the nearest railroad station, a distance of one hundred and fifty miles which took up eight days traveling in a sleigh, most of the way over the snow-covered mountains.

BAZIL'S MOTHER

The next day after I arrived here I went to the United States Indian office where a few aged Indians were assembled, the bulk of the tribes being absent on their annual winter buffalo hunt. Among those present was Bazil, one of the head-men, an aged and fine specimen of an Indian. I was introduced to Bazil by Dr. James Erwin, M. D., United States Agent in charge of the Shoshone reservation. Bazil was able to talk English brokenly; I was also told he could speak French. The Agent then took me to Bazil's camp, which was about a hundred yards or so from the office, to see an aged woman who was called by him, "Bazil's Mother."

She was seated on the ground in a tepee; her hair was gray and she had the appearance of being very old. Bazil said she was his mother and that she was about a hundred years old, "very old, very old."

Dr. Erwin alluded to her connection with the Lewis and Clark Expedition, and he seemed to be keenly interested in that fact. I was interested in the old woman because of her great age, for at that time I knew very little of the Lewis and Clark Expedition.

Bazil proved to be a very dutiful son to his mother. He was, in reality, only an adopted son and nephew. He cared for her tenderly and had his daughters and other women of the camp see to her every need. She was well provided for. The Agent issued her plenty of beef, flour, groceries and tobacco, which she liked to smoke. Her own son, Baptiste, alluded to by name by Captain Clark of the Expedition, lived about three miles above the agency at the foot of the mountains. I came to know him well later on.

THE BURIAL OF SACAJAWEA

On the morning of April ninth, the following year, I was told that Bazil's Mother had passed suddenly away during the night, in the log cabin that was in the camp, on her shake-down of quilts, blankets and pelts. The Agent had a coffin made for her, and he sent employees to dig her grave on the eastern slope of one of the foot-hills, a mile and one-half east of the agency where there were four graves of white people who were killed by hostile raiding Indians. This burial ground has been subsequently set apart by the Indian Office as a Shoshone Indian cemetery, but it still remains a part of the reservation. There are now several hundred Indian graves in it, thirty-seven of them being the graves of veteran Indian soldiers who served in the United States Army. The burial of Sacajawea took place late in the afternoon on the day on which she died. Those in attendance were her immediate relatives, the Agent and some of the employees. I read over her grave the Burial Service of the Episcopal Church. I little realized at the time that the heroine we laid to rest in years to come would become one of the outstanding women in American history. She sleeps with her face towards the dawn on the sunny slope of the Rocky Mountains. Her grave overlooks the beautiful Little Wind River Valley. Standing there we see close by the Shoshone Indian Mission school and, at a distance of about ten miles, the buildings of Fort Washakie. We see also, at about the same distance, the buildings of the former Shoshone Agency. Two miles further down the valley are the buildings of the government school. We see also the glistening waters of the Little Wind River and of Trout Creek, hurrying down the valley from this elevation of one mile above sea level towards their destination in the Gulf of Mexico. We see at the bottom of the valley, six miles off, great clouds of steam rising up from the famous Washakie Hot Springs. To the north, at a distance of seventy miles, arises the Washakie Needles, named in honor of the great Chief. To the south is the Beaver range of mountains. Far off to the east are the Owl Creek and Rattlesnake Mountains; and to the west, close by us, are the towering mountains of the main range of the Rockies, through the grim passes of which Sacajawea led the Expedition of 1805 and 1806, when no other guide was available who knew the Indian trails.

HER DESCENDANTS

Baptiste, Sacajawea's son, I knew over a period of some years up to his death. He had a large family. Those descendants now living are numerous. Baptiste lived on the reservation. He spent his time in hunting, fishing and selling Indian curios to supply the needs of his family. His grandchildren and great-grandchildren are living on the reservation. Baptiste made his home about three miles from the Shoshone Mission up to the time of his death. He died and was buried, according to the ancient custom of the Shoshones, in the rocks in a canyon west of the Mission at a distance of some seven miles at the head of Dry Creek.

From his rocky grave can be seen his mother's resting place, Sacajawea.

Baptiste's son, Wyt-te-gan, informed me one time that his father, Baptiste, had often told him that Baptiste's mother carried him (Baptiste) on her back when he was a baby, across the mountains when she led the first "Washington" across to the Great Waters towards the setting sun (Dab-be-dos-nank).

Bazil, the adopted son and nephew of Sacajawea and in whose camp she lived, died a few years after his mother. He was buried at a place about four miles from the Agency but was subsequently laid to rest beside the grave of Sacajawea, his adopted mother. Bazil was a noted pioneer guide, himself a great friend of Dr. Erwin who was Agent, resident of this reservation in the early seventies. His friend, Bazil, came to him, Dr. Erwin told me, and demanded permission from him to bring his mother's tent and pitch it close to Dr. Erwin's house. "For," said Bazil, "I am going away on a buffalo hunt and I want you to take special care of her, for she has been a great friend of the white people in the early days."

HER EXPERIENCE HATED BY HER PEOPLE

Sacajawea, during her life, never boasted of her journey and great service to the whites. In fact, on the other hand, she kept it secret for if the fact should have been published of her having led the Lewis and Clark Expedition it would have brought nothing but opprobrium and scorn from the members of her tribe. And Bazil would not have mentioned the fact to Dr. Erwin had he not been anxious for the welfare of his mother during his absence on the hunt.

Although Sacajawea was silent to the whites concerning her connection with the Lewis and Clark Expedition she used to amuse members of her family by relating to them some of her experiences during the journey. One time she told them that she had seen at the Great Waters toward the setting sun a fish as big as a log cabin. Captain Clark mentions the fact that they had a found a dead whale washed ashore when they reached the Pacific.

After Charboneau, her French mixed-blood husband's death, she was lost sight of to whites and Shoshones for many years while she was visiting kindred tribes of her people. She spent several years with the Comanches who are the same as Shoshones and speak the same language. But the homing instinct in her led her during her latter days to seek her own people in the mountains of Wyoming.

During the latter years of her life here she was known to the whites and Indians as Bazil's Mother. On my Parish Register of Burials, I recorded her burial under the date of April 9, 1884, as Bazil's Mother, Shoshone, age one hundred years. Date of death, April 9, Resident of Shoshone Agency. Cause of death, old age. Place of burial, burial grounds Shoshone Agency. Signature of Clergyman, John Roberts. She was also known to the Indians by other names according to the Shoshone custom, as: Wadze-Wipe, the Lost Woman; Booe-nive, Grass Maiden; Bah-Ribo, Water White Man.

**